THE WILL

Louis McCray
The Will

Published by Spines
ISBN: 979-8-89569-137-3

THE WILL

LOUIS MCCRAY

1

Dang, these machines never work around here anymore, said Mr Jeff, owner of the Low Price Laundromat in the South Bronx Area. I have to call my mechanic every other day which is costing me a fortune. 12 dryers and 14 washing machines all not worth a damn. I tell you I should've listened to my grandfather and bought that cab service company when I had the chance. Now every little dollar I get goes right back into fixing the business and staying afloat. Rent is crazy and if my wife has another kid, I'm gonna kill her Jimmy. Jimmy is a tenant in apartment 4B in the building over the laundromat. Listen, Mr Jeff if you keep sticking it in she's definitely gonna keep popping them out. I mean that is how sex works when you're married for 35 years, 37 but who's counting, said Mr Jeff. I got 4 bad ass grown no good kids and they all cost me 100 thousand each at least. I'm stressed out my mind brother, what I would give to be on a beach in the middle of the Bahamas sipping on a coconut looking at some fine young tenderonis running into that clear ocean water with them tight thongs up the crack of that,

A, A, Mr Jeff come on now this is a place of business, your business which is none of my business but I get your point. Work is tough even at my spot at the Bank, doing Security to watch other people transfer funds. I ain't got all day with their stupid smiles when they leave with a fat envelope under their jacket or tucked in their pants. I feel like calling my boys to meet them before they get in their cars and bus them in the head but I'm a man of the Lord now, no more criminal thoughts. I did 5 years and I'm not going back for chump change.

Chump change adds up my boy believe me if these machines can stay working i can stack some change in my piggy bank for real.

Well get some new joints because your dryer number 7 stays robbing me. It only gets hot when the sun comes through the window between 1 and 3 o'clock in the summertime. I swipe my card and put it on extra hot then I tell your son to call me before going to school in the morning, come down and my shit still be wet, Mr Jeff.

You can always hang your clothes up in your bathroom like back in my day. We had the tub bucket and hanging pens. That's all you needed, put your clothes up in the morning, open the windows and by the time your moms cooked dinner with the oven making the house hot, "Bing," your draws are done.

I ain't got time for that old man with your 1964 remedies, said Jimmy!

That's your problem young buck, you want to cry

about money but never want to improvise. Yall kids waste money like you ll trying to die today. Like it's no tomorrow.

Excuse me Sir ain't you running a business here?

Yes but I still dry my draws in my bathroom to keep a clean pair on deck for when my little honey dip wants to slide on over and lick, lick, lick on this lollipop.

You're a nasty old Fart Mr Jeff how old are you anyway, 65?

62, but I like em in the 29-32 area. They have been there but they ain't done what I'm about to do to um, and that's a guarantee young no bucks.

Give me my bag of clothes imma be late for work messing with you. Tell Junior to call me in the morning for my last load, fucking dryer number 7.

Tell him yourself, your secretary must be off today, said Mr Jeff as he proceeded to go clean the restroom in the back he yelled, BETTY, stop stealing my soap, I see you I got eyes all over this place,

Please Mr Jeff you always think someone is taking something in this raggedy ass place, I don't need your soap you old buzzard, fix your machines and stay out of my business...

Jimmy goes into his building, 555 Southern Boulevard passing a couple of weed connoisseurs. God damn fellas that shit strong as shit, let me hit that Willow? A young high school student that lives on the 2nd floor always hanging in the building with his goonies doing God knows what. Stays with his mother that can't control him and a little brother that's not far from a weed head himself.

Yo Jim, said Willow you can't handle the truth fool. Hit

this and I'm not responsible for the outcome but I'll take good care of yea girl Debbie after your funeral..

And i'll beat your little ass from my grave yeah little fucker take that shit in your house, theirs old people that live on the first floor that stay complaining. They can't smell your crackhead weed, going through their windows and under their doors, you're gonna kill them with your stupid little dumb ass. You'll be lucky they don't call them boys. All they're gonna do is give us a ticket or tell us to move, so scared, said Willow as he blew out his smoke into the hallway, disregarding Jimmy's warning like he always does. This is my block!

All the goonies laughed as Jimmy continued to walk past to his 4 floor walk up that he's been dealing with the past 2 years he had his crib.

I'm so tired of this building as he finally made it to his door with his half dry laundry.

O Hi babe, said Debbie as he entered his one bedroom apartment to the smell of spaghetti and meatballs, one of his favorite dinners ever that Debbie loves to cook for him. I'm trying to finish your dinner before you bounce for work tonight. I KNOW you love my cooking, go take your shower while I get the table ready.

On one condition, said Jimmy!

Put the food on low and come get in this shower with me, deal or no deal.

Deal, said Debbie, I got you! I work early in the morning so I won't see you until I get home around 6 o'clock. I got to give meds all day so if you don't get it now tomorrow I'm going to be sleepy as hell. That's why I'm making enough spaghetti for 2 days.

As Jimmy leads her to the shower, Does Willow hit on you?

That young boy that be making noise on the roof like he is making rap videos, him and his friends be saying little flirty shit but they're harmless, Why?

Let me know if I need to beat his ass? You still got your mace and stun gun i brought u, Debbie started laughing but Jimmy was serious as fuck. He's a smart ass that's all and I don't trust him and his little minions all threw this building like they were top flight security. They need to be in school or studying or something.

That's great step daddy but right now you need to be studying this ass. Get in this shower before the food burns up and you gotta leave before you eat.

O imma eat alright, said Jimmy.

So nasty, you know you love me baby.

START YOU PIECE OF SHIT, Start

Wroom, Wroom

There you go baby, said Jimmy as he tried continuously to start his 2004 Z100 Tahoe Truck, white with cream interior. It's 2023 so this 3 owner 19 year old truck has taken his toll but it's still alive and kicking somewhat. Racing to Manhattan, I-95 South towards The George Washington Bridge to merge to the West Side HighWay trying to get to his Security Job at Chase Bank on 51 and 6th Ave. Doing

Security for Effective hasn't been all it was cracked up to be. It was a ruff start getting put on by his Ex-Con cousin Mannie. They both signed up at the same time for the Company but Mannie couldn't find all the paperwork he needed to get hired so Jimmy got on. First he had to do an 16 hour course to get his certificate that was split up into 2 days of video torture and applications. Then he had to buy some black pants with black work shoes, non-refundable. Finally they gave him a tight ass blue Security shirt with a badge that made him look like a fake airplane pilot.

2

Jimmy bounced around to a few sites the first few weeks. He secured Macy's, and a hospital which he loved, that's where he met Debbie, a few lunch break convos and he got them digits, a few dates and he got those draws, next thing you know she started leaving clothing at his crib letting all his thots know there's a new Queen B in town. Jimmy didn't mind that he fell head over heels for her and they've been inseparable ever since. They got caught in one of the doctors' break rooms making out that's what caused Jimmy to be transferred to the Bank. They gave Debbie a second chance because she was the best nurses-aid they had in 12 years.

Finally making it to his sight after arguing with the parking lot guy because he misplaced his parking pass he suckered his Site Director into giving him for a discount on parking.

Yo Bro, said Eric the morning guard. What time are you supposed to be here, 5 o'clock right? Well it's 5:15 and

I'm late now to pick up my daughter from her dance class. I'm gonna have to take a 40 dollar Uber again so my wife won't threaten to poison my food or kill me in my sleep.

She's very abusive, said Jimmy! You should leave her before it's too late, take your daughter and run because it's obvious she doesn't love you Bro.

No, you need to get here 10 minutes ahead of time like it says in the rule book to relieve your man, who is me dickhead. I'm out and I'm not running anything down, you figure out what to do tonight on your own. I would say peace but i don't like you, wait till you get a kid, I'm coming later than a mug.

Fuck you very much!

Language, Language, what does it say in the rule book about saying Fuck on duty.

IM OFF DUTY 20 minutes ago, yeah Kumquat!

KUMQUAT, you've been eaten squid again smells like vagina and cream soda over here, don't kiss your daughter with that breath.

Fuck you, said Eric as he made a running exit threw the revolving doors.

Jimmy fixed his uniform attire and proceeded to scale the lobby of the bank.

A few people were in line, not too much traffic so he started his shift by signing the logbook and checking the bathrooms, then the waiting area. He asked the window clerks if they were cool, then stood at his post by the exit doors to control the flow.

He had 4 hours before his half an hour break.

Things were going smooth until he had to check some

skateboarders jumping off the company sign outside in front of the building.

Listen kids, take your boards up the street before I take them and put them in my office closet. 2 of the kids took off but one tried to go for one more jump. Jimmy beat him to the sign and stood in the way,

Fuck You yeah fake ass cop!

I get off at 12 midnight, come back around that time and ill put my 12 inch shoe up your backside, No Diddy!

The skateboarder threw him the finger as he caught up to his boys.

Im a fuck somebody up today, said Jimmy to himself as he went back into the bank clearly with an attitude. The next three hours were hard, Jimmy was dying to go smoke like he usually does during break time down the block next to the loading dock of the MARRIOTT Hotel. He found a little cut spot to blow it down. It's not that much traffic at 9 o'clock on his street and he knew everyone from the pizza shop to the office building on the opposite corner. Everyone knew Jimmy, some even came to meet him at his spot to smoke a cigarette or talk weed Scientifics from strains to best spot to cop from.

9 o'clock, cut time as Jimmy told the staff he'd be back in a half. Bring me a sneaker bar said, Miss Helen the head bank teller who had a ten year run at the same bank. No problem Miss Helen, blunt in hand. Jimmy sparked his gonja as soon as he hit the doors. Walking to his spot he heard, Yuuup!

Yuuup! It was Arty, an African hustler that worked the

block selling bags, glasses, headphones, wallets, a real slick talker that smoked every chance he got.

I see you big dog, going to break, I smelled that trash weed from down the block.

Fuck you mean dummy, said Jimmy. I smoke the finest herbals known to man, you be smoking that plant based doctor weed from Ghana, your moms be sending you in rice bags. I don't even have time for your BS today Arty, spark up or go back up the street with your brothers before the leather starts peeling off them fake Gucci bags and you have to pick up another load.

I make more money then you

I get more sex then you dirt boy, ask Nina said Jimmy coughing frantically off his smoke.

Nina is Artys' aunt back home that Jimmy is in love with. She comes back and forth every time her visa expires. She's the plug connecting all her peoples with the Chinese traders on Canal St, and Chinatown

My Aunt loves African Mandingos not American Frank footers, said Arty with his African accent. They both started busting out in laughter as Jimmy checked his Cell Phone for the time.

Gotta run to the store to get Miss Helen a Damn sneaker, she knows I only have a half, she is too lazy to go get her own snacks.

Run Forest, Run said, Arty catch you later, Player hater.

Jimmy pulled out his little baby bottle of Febreeze to hide all the weed smells from the spot. He gave Miss

Helen her chocolate bar as he busted down his Snapple apple and bag of Doritos before going back to his post

10 o'clock hit and it was time for all the employees to go home and shut down the inside part of the Bank, only leaving the ATM machines that Jimmy had to guard on the outer section of the bank until 12 midnight.

It was time to call his Baby Debbie after Helen locked up and everyone went home for the night.

3

Hello, boy you know I gotta get up early to give meds said Debbie. Everyone went home, did you touch Miss Helen's ass again, you know she wants you that's why she be rolling her eyes at me when I come to bring you dinner with her old cougar ass.

Is that Hate I hear, I didn't say anything when that Doctor, what's his name? Doctor Dowinsky tried to line me up for an Orchidectomy. He told my doctor I wanted to be a Transgender just so I couldn't get you pregnant and reproduce.

We only went out one time, said Debbie.

But you kissed him didn't you, you kissed him with my lips and tried to lie. Luckily i'm a genius, something told me not to go to my appointment that day. You and Winsky tried to line me up.

Ain't nobody tried to line you stupid, you told me we weren't working to go out and find my match remember.

I don't recall that conversation at all, I told you I had

too much Red Bull and Henny. You know how I get when I'm on that HENNY TRAIN. I always tell you to do your thing, cause imma do my thing and everything will be everything.

Shut up, said Debbie, tired and annoyed of this old conversation. I'm going back to bed, you're gonna make me late in the morning.

Wait, wait, wait, what do you got on?

Nothing, said Debbie. I just got in the bed after the shower and finished what you started, Mr I gotta go.

You naked, said Jimmy.

Send me a picture real quick!

By Jim, see you tomorrow I don't have time for this fool.

No she didn't, said Jim as Debbie ended the call. 5 seconds later, boom Debbie's clean shaved sweetness all over Jimmy's cell phone with hearts and kisses before he could hit redial.

Drooling over his woman's sweet nectar Jimmy started to hear a noise coming from one of the 4 ATM machines he was guarding. He noticed that the second to last one looked like it was malfunctioning, ringing off and lighting up like a 4 of July commercial. He gave a closer look as the noise stopped and the screen cleared back to normal with a message. We are preparing your cash. 2 seconds later a money counting sound started and the money box opened up displaying a watt of Blue Face hundreds. Jimmy's mouth dropped to the ground as he looked into the camera and reached for the money that damn near spit out the machine.

All kinds of things were racing through his head at this point. It was late so no customers were in sight and the machine closed back up leaving him with money in hand. Jimmy quickly slid over to the counter putting his back toward the camera as he counted the cash. 7,500 dollars, this gotta be a trick, should I mark it down and return it tomorrow, Is this a blessing from God?

Should I call it in? Daddy does need a new pair of shoes, or a vacation to Cancun. Imma put this in my pocket, bring it tomorrow, if someone says something i'll turn it in and tell them the truth, they got the footage. I got this!

A few more late night ATM drawers came in using the third machine that had the malfunction and there were no problems. In and out like normal, a couple of short conversations and goodnights and it was finally 12 o'clock shut down time. Jim quickly shut the bank Doors made sure the coast was clear, then boogied to the parking lot to get his V. He wanted to call Deebie so bad but he knew a curse out would definitely happen. Fuck it he dipped home, threw his work close on the couch with the money in it, jumped in the shower woke Deb up for work dying to tell her but he knew his girl would trip so he held back his little secret till he felt he was in the clear.

Debbie Got up made her some coffee and as soon as Jimmy's head hit the pillow she begged him to go get a Bronx breakfast, Yes a traditional bacon, egg, and cheese. I could feel my readers smiling because yall know that's a hit in the hood.

Come on now you know im tired as fuck said Jimmy,

you know its gonna take me a half an hour to get my face done so go get it, Debbie commanded.

Why you gotta look so damn good, it's just work, Jimmy shouted.

A bunch of old ass biddies checking you out.

Don't get slapped, wait till you get old and need someone to take care of you, you're gonna wish something this fine comes in and wipe your stink ass, Hurry up!

Jimmy threw on his sweats and went for his keys and money forgetting about the knot of cash moving fast he ended up dropping all the money on his living room floor. God damn it he said to himself as he picked it all up before Debbie came out the bathroom to see what all the commotion was.

Hurry the fuck up, you could say please, im tired too!

Pleaseeeee, said Debbie sarcastically as Jimmy found twenty of his own cash and hit the door.

This bodega is always crowded because they make the best food and Mommy that runs the place got the fattest BBL you could ever see. The Mexicans are buying cases and drinking in the store just to watch her walk back and forth. He even caught Mr Jeff in there tryna get a squeeze or 2 with his nasty old ass. Women are extra hugging too, I dont know which way mommy swings but somebody getting the action park ride of their life, let me tell you, on God!

Hi mommy, how are you feeling this morning?

Good papi and yourself?

With her dominican accent gets me everytime, stand

down boy not now as Jimmy grabbed his manhood and ordered.

Let me get 2 bacon, egg & cheese mommy.

A little Salt and pepper on one, I know how you like it papi

Stand down, Stand down, YES mommy, please and thank you!

When mommy behind the counter turned to get the food she gave Jim the view he was looking for.

My Dear Jesus, looks like 2 earths colliding. Let me get up out of this store. He grabbed the bag turned around to reach for the door and ran straight into Debbie.

This is what's taking you so long, give me my damn sandwich about to make me late.

Want me to drive you, said Jimmy.

Nuh I want you to get out of mommy's ass and take your ass in the house, nobody wants you but me. Your muva told me how many times she dropped you on your head. Your father still calls you, Can't Get Right from the movie Life.

Ha Ha Ha, u got a smart ass mouth, one day imma pay a Bum to hit you in the back of the head take your breakfast and beat you with it.

And that's the day you're gonna wake up dead, said Debbie running toward the train.

How I'm gonna wake up dead, YOU CRAZY ASS!

4

Racing up the steps to count the cash again, Jimmy texted Eric who should be at work by now. Hit me back, fool . I want to know if anyone is talking about the close last night. I think I forgot to check if the main door was locked and I don't want no smoke, so hit me back asap!

Jimmy layed down to sleep but he couldn't, now the stress was pouring on and he was getting nervous about losing his job.

Finally Eric texts him back,

All Good bro just have your ass on time today.

Jimmy texted back, i'll be there early, I promise you.

I did it, nothing happened now how I'm gonna tell Deb about this money?

2:30 Jimmy alarm rang from the charger.

Up, let's go old bones, as Jim hit the bathroom, to freshen up, ironed his uniform and ordered chinese food for Deb so she could eat when she gets in at six. He hid the extra cash in his sneaker box and put it under the bed. He wanted to move real early to see if he could nip any buzzing that was in the air from the night before. Plus he had to get in the office to see what the cameras really caught.

Debbie has been a nurse's assistant for 6 years at Mount Sinai Hospital. She loves her job, got three raises and employee of the month for a year straight. She works the inpatients on 2 different floors and the emergency room to keep busy and make the time fly. She has sent a lot of people home and has seen a lot of them get sick and pass. That's why she loves Jimmy so much he listens to all her tribes and tribulations. He even sings love songs to her to soothe her nightmares and trauma. From Babyface to Johnny Gill, Jim is even hitting the high notes to make her laugh all her pain away. He used to sing at church as a kid, His parents Gwen and James got stories for days and they love them some Debbie for their only son.

They wanted Jim to have a singing career but he chose the streets and ended up doing 3 years at Rikers Island fighting a gun charge his cousin got him involved with, finally getting released he lost all his music contacts and needed a job badly. It was construction or Security. And you know what happened next.

Debbie was doing her last run checking on a few patients before she clocked out for the day. She had two more meds to give, one blood drawing and finally a sponge bath for Mr Gibson. Mr Gibson is a 65 year old retired accountant but he still got it going on. Covid almost took him out in 2020 now he's back in for heart surgery, he was recovering well until it was a few complications so they ran tests on him and he's been in the hospital under Debbie's care for the last 2 weeks.

Mr Gibson loves to get his sponge bath from Debbie he won't take it from anyone else. He loves her professionalism and how she takes her time, long story short Mr Gibson is a freak and he gets off when Debbie washes his private parts.

Hey Mr. Gibson, how are you feeling today, said Debbie.

I'm about to feel 10 times better once we get started, I'm a dirty man, real dirty said Mr Gibson sarcastically

Now Mr Gibson im not going through this with you today, imma report you to my Bosses and tell your wife how you are flashing me Sir. That's not gentleman like and you persuaded yourself to be a gentleman when I first met you.

Mr Gibson wasn't trying to hear anything; he quickly exposed his third leg to Debbie and it wasn't a game. Mr Gibson was packing a baby thigh and Debbie was taken back how solid this old man was and ready.

Mr Gibson pulled out 300 dollars out of his wallet by the bed and placed Debbie hand on his partner forcing her hand to go up and down his snake. He took the sponge and soaped his stomach letting the suds run down his body to make the situation nice and wet. Then he pulled the curtains closed like they normally have it when he's getting bathed.

Debbie wasn't new to this situation, she usually just switched clients when they flirted with her but Mr Gibson was a smooth talking OG, that looked like he had a lot of cash.

Just let it happen naturally, no harm no foul, I appreciate your hard work and skill said Mr Gibson

I see how hard it is too, said Debbie, kind of admiring Mr Gibson's bold actions. Kinda turned her on she even grabbed her titty as she caught herself. Ten minutes felt like an hour as Mr Gibsons let loose in the bucket as Debbie jerked it all out. She quickly changed her gloves and dried Mr Gibson off then put the room back in order before she opened the curtains and poured the water out in the bathroom toilet.

Damn this old dude almost filled up this bucket, how many kids he got Jesus. Debbie, get a hold of yourself girl. Jimmy's gonna kill my ass, I can not believe this day.

By the time she went back to check on Mr Gibson he was fast asleep and another 200 dollars was on his night stand. Debbie grabbed it, tucked her money away and went to the break area to regroup. Fantasies of her taking Mr Gibson's baseball bat for three innings had her sweating. She needed some ice cold water, clock out then get the hell up outta there. .

As soon as she got to the break room boom she ran smack into big mouth Crystal. Crystal, a dark skinned young half asian, half black, short and thick co-worker that plays both sides and has been on Debbies heels for years. Crystal can read something up before you could say Hello, Goodbye! What's going on Miss Debbie?

Hey Crystal how you doing girl, How LONG was your day, was it HARD? I mean anybody JERK you around today Dr Arnal is tripping he is trying to get me to do overtime but I need some rest. Tomorrows gonna be another LONG HARD day for me. I'm outta here!

Before Crystal could say alright girl, Debbie headed to the lockers for her purse and clocked out.

Debbie, Debbie hold up dang your cellphone girl you left it on the table in the break room, slow down before you lose something else, said Crystal. Like that fine ass man of yours, Jimmy.

What Bitch!

Not today, don't get beat up, like real bad, real quick too.

I'm just playing with you dang take your panties out your big butt, said Crystal you know its a man shortage. Girls just want to have fun.

Where are we going with this? I gotta get home tryna give MY MAN some before he goes to work.

I hear that hot shit, ain't nothing let's go out, Double date or something. Well talk, set something up if it aint a problem, said Crystal.

No problem at all, haven't been out in a while sounds like fun, said Debbie.

Could be a lot of fun, said Crystal. Well see what's up, get it poppin, get drunk, make it clap. I got a spot to shake the dust off that ass.

You a fucking mess, tommorrow I'll have a clear head and we can chop it up, cool.

Cool, said Crystal, laters!

5

Jimmy texted Debbie he was leaving for work early and he brought Chinese food for her to eat. How much he loved her and how he couldn't wait to see her again. Debbie didn't even notice she was still tryna break up with Mr Gibson's penis she kept putting on hand sanitizer the whole ride home. She couldn't even eat. She made herself a hot bath, grabbed her favorite toy and released it. All the tension from the day and Mr Gibson had her so horny, then Crystal hitting on her again. It was a G spot mission in full effect, Yes LORD!

Jimmy made it to work earlier than expected. So early Eric almost passed out and knocked down all the line dividers in the bank. Jimmy laughed it off but stayed focused, he went to Miss Helen and asked her directly if everything was copasetic. Did anything strange happen this morning, you know Eric is a little slow and he's not Top flight like me.

Miss Helen laughed and said, no everything is going

pretty smoothly today our numbers are correct people been doing more deposits than anything and the cameras gonna get fixed in 2 weeks we had to get a new contractor the old system had glitches we have to rewire the whole system may take a month to be up and running. I only told you and Eric the rest of the staff can't know they may start to get sticky fingers. Keep your eyes on Tanisha and Thomas. I think they are having an affair and imma have to transfer one of them until the system is back up and running.

Whattttt, said Jimmy so the cameras are out, Okay, Okay! Anything else I need to know before I send Eric home for the night.

No, just have an extra eye. We're gonna be loaded because we can't get any cash pick ups. The systems have to be up and running for everyone's safety, especially the armed guards.

Jimmy reported this information to Eric and sent him home.

I just got away with 7500 cash, nooooo! I'm taking my baby to Cancun and can't wait to tell her on my break.

Jimmy kept looking at that ATM machine that spit out the cash, everyone was using it and it seemed to be working just fine. So that's it, it was smooth sailing.

Break time Jimmy didn't even smoke, he went to Ray's Pizza shop in the middle of the block. Slice wasn't as good as the hood but if you're hungry 2 with pepperoni and extra cheese can hit the spot. Jimmy sat down and called Debbie who was in ecstasy after her bath, wink wink.

HEY baby, said Debbie i'm sorry I didn't call you after

your text i was so tired my day was LONG and HARD. Let me tell you.

Hold that thought I got even better news for you, said Jimmy. We are off to CANCUN BABY!

I got a bonus from my job, It finally came. I didn't want to tell you about it until I was sure I'd get it. It was between me and Eric and they gave me 5000 dollars so imma use it for us to take a much needed vacation. So thongs and suntan lotion or naked we can just stay naked for 2 weeks on the beach. I know I'm bigger than the Mexicans, they can't see me, right?

Hell no they can't see you baby, with Mr Gibson on the back of her mind, WE OUT THIS BITCH! Finally we're gonna use these passports we've been sitting on for 2 years now, said Debbie. Imma get on line and book and find the perfect spot, i'm excited. Yeah we need this so bad you did it BABY!

Jimmy, imma eat and hit you later, I love you so much!

I love you more, imma order my swimsuits, my hats, i need a new beach bag, its going down.

What was your news Baby?

O nothing a friend of mine wants to double date, you know Crystal hot ass, we can make it a celebration, a vacation go away party, said Debbie, good stuff, see you later, mwahhh!

Jimmy scarfed down his pizza and drank his favorite Snapple apple. Tomorrow is both him and Debbie's day off together and they had some planning to do.

. . .

OKAY GOOD NIGHT MISS HELEN, Peace everybody, it's 2 Uber's outside waiting for you guys. Get home safe people.

Now it's time to secure these crazy ass ATMs out here spitting out thousands of dollars. Happy to have gotten away with it Jimmy was trying to put last night in his back pocket. 2 old ladies came in to use the machines and Jimmy had to help them step by step to pull out 40 dollars so they could split 20 each. Then a few more people came in and none of them used the third ATM that let the money rain last night.

It was about 11:26 and Jimmy was thinking about nothing but watching ass on the beach with sunglasses on, hiding his wandering eyes from Debbie, then the fireworks happened again. The box opened and Jimmy pulled out another knot, much more than the first dropping some on the floor. He was so nervous and shocked that this happened again. He filled both his pockets up with loot. One more person came in before he locked the doors and counted 12,000 dollars.

!2,000, the cameras aren't working and if he reported this Eric would laugh his ass off and call him all kinds of disrespectful obscenities and that's after he calls him dumb, then ask for PC before he tells. Eric would never turn in free money. He's a big fan of finders keepers, Jimmy dropped 5 dollars and Eric stepped on it right in front of him and didn't give it back. Who told you to drop it playa, if you drop money you don't need it, Thank You!

Jimmy took the cash home and put it in his sneaker box

with the other 7,500. That's 19,500, 500 short of 20 thou-sand in 2 days. What the FUCK, said Jimmy waking up Debbie who probably just finish riding Mr Gibsons horse dong in her dreams.

Wiping saliva from her mouth and cold out her eyes. WHAT. "Is everything alright? said Debbie.

Yeah, yeah babe go back to sleep, I:m sorry I just stubbed my toe on the bed.

Come to bed baby I know you're tired.

Nuh baby i'll be back imma go outside and get me a beer, you want something?

Yes, bring me back some spicy Doritos and a pack of Raisinets, mwahhh!

Jimmy had a lot on his mind, He needed someone to talk to so he went to the store then ended up in the Laun-dromat with Mr Jeffs oldest son Junior, JR for short.

What's up Jimmy let me get one of those beers playa, Modelo Nigro must be your favorite. I always see you sipping on these bad boys, said Jr.

Yeah man, I went to the bar with my cousin one time and he ordered this and it's been my choice ever since. Better than Coors, Bud and Heinekens to me.

You left some clothes to wash or something, what do I owe the honor of your presence?

Nothing man cant sleep, came across a situation and when I get in situations they don't usually end well for me. I don't want to get back into it with the law and I can't afford to lose my job. I just got a funny feeling something bad is gonna happen at the end of my rainbow. Life has so many twists and turns to it. Nothing comes easy and not to tell all my business something has fallen in my lap and I hope it stops because I don't know if I can stop taking it.

Listen, who all knows about this situation, how many people have you told, said Jr?

No one, this is the first time I'm talking about it with you.

Well leave it in God's hands, put it like this he got you in this situation so leave it up to him to get you out. Some things happen to good people, they call them blessings. If God blesses you with something my brother just try to do the right thing with it. Do what your heart tells you to do, and when it comes to them boys. You don't know nothing, you ain't seen nothing, you ain't hear nothing even if they got a little bit of evidence. It wasn't you, say it with me, IT WASN'T ME!

IT WASN'T ME, said Jimmy with confidence in his voice.

They drink 2 more beers and Jimmy finally cooled his head enough to go to bed in peace.

Thanks JR, how old are you man?

I'm 27 but I've been through some things, this is the hood nobody gets through clean bro!

Facts, said Jimmy Facts!

Debbie woke up refreshed as she shook yesterday off ready to do some online shopping as she put on her Travel agent hat to Bookit.com. Got the round trip tickets JetBlue with 2 week stay at the Hilton Resort All-inclusive, everything came up to $5,200 hundred dollars she woke Jimmy up to confirm and lock it in. Everything was a go, as she jumped on Jimmy and started giving him a plethora of kisses. They have been waiting to get out of the country for so long. NYC is like a big ass hamster wheel that is so hard to jump off of with all the hustle and bustle. This is a well deserved vacation that they can't wait to go on.

Jimmy gave up his credit card and Debbie gave up her assets. Just a little sample of what's gonna happen when I get you to Cancun. How's your Hispanic, imma need you, said Jimmy I know money not language BABY!

I got you daddy, we gonna have hella fun, I already ordered some easy to take off string bikini outfits, bring your elephant draws the ones I love. Imma do my squats and work these thighs in the gym, we got 2 weeks before take off time, so call your job I don't want to hear about no replacement issues, or Eric can't cover a shift. Make sure they call in some temps today.

Debbie was not playing at all; she didn't want nothing or no one to mess up her get away.

Jimmy called right away and since he had the dates and the cash he got everything locked in for the trip, Debbie had so much vacation time she planned to take off a month so she could really feel like she got the time off she deserved.

Shop, then sex, shop then sex, They ordered a large pie, then Netflix and chilled.

Jimmy was watching Beverly Hills Cop 5, cuddling with his girl, but in the back of his mind when 11 o'clock hit. Will the ATM machine ring off again? Who's working tonight? I'm probably missing out on some big money. He damn near wanted to drive to his job to see.

It is what it is and Jimmy had to let it go. Debbie had to go to work to put in her time so she went to bed leaving Jimmy up to Netflix by himself since he works in the evening.

6

When Jimmy woke in the morning, Debbie was already gone to work. He made some coffee and decided to go to Fordham Rd to get some white Air force Ones, boxers, white tees and tank tops for the trip. He was actually looking forward to it more than Debbie. He went to jail, got out and jumped straight to work. The only trip they had was a drive to Atlanta to visit Debbie's sister for her niece's birthday party slash graduation. They tore the hotel down 2 nights thow, drinking gambling with her sister's friends and a big pool party that the cops broke up because of the pound of weed Jimmy brought down. He didn't want to be copping trash from dudes he didn't know. So he came packing, giving everyone in the Hotel weed so he didn't drive back with any. The state troopers in VA were on him but they let him go by the skin of his teeth.

When he got back in the crib he called Eric,

Yo, yo, yo, who worked my shift last night was everything copacetic.

Why do you keep checking in on me about this stupid ass job,Son. I took off today, enjoying my time with my family, said Eric. Call the office. I think they sent out a temp named Harold, perfect guard name Harold. Harold said Freeze sucker.

They both laughed.

You should see him when you go in because he came back and did my morning shift so you tell me what he's like, fool, PEACE!

Jimmy went into work like he regularly does, Harold greeted him at the door. A little older chubby man looked like Carl from Family Matters.

So you're the Top Flight Security Guard I've been hearing so much about. Mr. Jimmy, PAUSE NO Diddy, that's what these kids are saying now-a-days. All of them be Diddy Boppin to me.

Jimmy laughed

Nuh, Mr. Figaroa to be exact, Jimmy Figaroa to be clear and you are Harold correct.

How's the shifts been going? Anything out of the ordinary has happened since yesterday, said Jimmy wanting to know if any missing money talk has arised.

No it's been cool, Miss Helen has been great and her staff, much respect, I like this sight. I actually heard I'll be covering for you on your 2 week vaca, where to?

Cancun, yeah me and my lady Debbie out of here.

Well enjoy it, said Harold any chance you get to get out of New York City take it.

Imma say a few words to that fine ass Miss Helen see if

i could get those digits. Yeah them 7 digits, I needs that. I'm saying it right, young Blood?

Yeah you on point Big Dog go get that, Jimmy looked at Miss Helen Sponge Bob body and syringed at the thought of her and Harold bumping and grinding. He organized his area and got the line moving, as it was a little crowded today being a Friday evening and all. People were cashing checks and paying debts clearing up that spending money for the weekend. Miss Helen informed him that the cameras were still out after Harold finished squeezing her up by the deposit slips counter.

I think he macked that number thought Jimmy as he went to clean around the ATM machines, He touched the third machine and uttered, you ain't been acting up I see. Maybe the glitches stopped, I guess I will see what happens tonight. Wiped them down and proceeded to do a full sweep of the bathrooms. Courteously escorted a few old people out the door then break time.

Jimmy was walking to his spot when he smelled that African dirt weed. ARTY why the fuck you over here in my spot smoking that bullshit again.

Listen it's free, im drinking tiger bone and im higher then yo silly ass.

What up Jimmy, what's popping, my brother, my cousin, my son? The 2 embraced each other with a pound.

Why are you drinking Tiger Bone, that's chinese, you don't know your african do you, said Jimmy.

My man Chin be giving me shots of this shit when I pick up my bags, I kinda fell in love with the shit, you want some.

Jimmy took a shot and sparked up his high grade, That bull. That GG.

Arty started coughing, damn son!

Yeah this not for kids Ghana, that's why you shouldn't be in my spot, Lungsmackers only, I know you be smelling my shit from around the corner and manhattan blocks is long as fuck.

Yeah yo shit be wicked! You should bring me a pound, you know how I got down out here.

I know you be getting locked up, you mean. Every week the cops are running you up outta here they stay taking your stash, I ain't got time for that, said Jimmy with disgust.

I heard you're gonna be gone for 2 weeks to Cancun, said Arty.

Eric's mouth is bigger than the Grand Canyon, what else he told you.

You and Miss Helen had a thing a couple years back, you used to massage her feet?

Hell nuh, what the fuck, said Jimmy.

I hope you out her when me and Eric shoot the five, wait till I call him today, be out here imma put the beats on him, I may lose my job behind this one.

Im just fucking with you, said Arty.

I'm out, break time is up, fool. Do yourself a favor and throw the rest of that trash away.

Yeah aight, said Arty as he quickly grabbed for his cell phone to make a phone call and proceeded back up the block to his stash spot where he hid his big duffle bag of accessories for the low-low.

Jimmy went back inside after he cleaned himself up. He broke up a situation with a teller and a consumer that felt he was waiting in line a little too long. He was in a rush because he was on the clock handling personal business. The tellers in his mind were taking too long and he seriously needed to withdraw some serious cash. Boy went crazy, screaming and yelling causing a scene like a toddler wanting some candy.

Jimmy swung into action putting the man into a submission hold after trying to talk some sense into him to calm down and relax. He followed all the steps then he threw the guy into a head lock after he tried to swing on him in the middle of the waiting area.

Jimmy escorted the guy out to the front and persuaded him to leave before he went to jail and not only did he not handle his business for the day, but may also lose his job altogether.

Your right, your right as the man calmed down and took off running back to his office when he realized that time wasn't on his side.

Jimmy was happy to escape a lot of paperwork and reports.

After making sure the guest and the staff were okay, Jimmy stood back at his post just in case anything else broke out. He can pretty much visually control the room from that area.

7

10 o'clock came and went and Jimmy was finally alone with his money machines until 12.

People were coming and going like normal, no real alarm ringing activities, until quarter to closing. Jimmy was happy to close without any mishaps The lighting show started again. This time on not one but the last two of the last 2 machines. The money boxes opened up and cash just started flying out of both ATMs like a baller throwing money on a stripper.

Jimmy didn't know what to do; he just locked the doors and started holding his head. He kicked frantically putting the cash in one pill, looking out into the street to see if anyone noticed what was going on in the bank as the ATMs went back to their normal screens.. He quickly scooped the money up and put it in his backpack.

Jimmy was sweating, heart pounding a mile a minute. He took his water bottle out the side of his work bag and drank it all in one gulp. All he could think about was going back to jail on a bank robbery charge this time. He clocked out then secured the bank doors were locked then ran to the parking lot. Jumped in his truck then turned the AC to full blast as he tried to calm the hell down.

Grabbing his phone he was thinking to call Debbie and tell her all about it but for some reason he called his mother Gwen.

Gwen answered his calls any and every time, she loved her baby that much.

Hi Jim momma's baby, what do I owe this honor early this morning, said Gwen.

Ma I don't know you know me. I think I just wanted to hear your voice before I rode home, just got off of work and I was feeling a little irritable.

Is everything alright with little miss Debbie?

Yeah mom, she's fine. we're actually getting ready to go on vacation finally after all these years of grinding. We off to Cancun Mexico for tequila and tacos.

That sounds like fun, don't you take nothing in your bag that can get you behind bars.

Jimmy looked at his work bag as she said that.

You know what almost happened to you on that drive down south. You don't need that kind of trouble in your life at this day and time, said Momma Gwen.

Jimmy confirmed nothing like that would be going on as he asked her to just pray for him and Debbie's safe journey. He really was asking for prayer for the trouble he was bringing upon himself with that bank money in his bag.

He talked to his mother all the way home as her voice eased his mind.

Debbie was doing an overnight so he just texted her he was taking it down as he sat back in his living room counting all that cash.

When he was done he counted out 40,000 dollars. He never ever had that much money in hand at one time. He knew for sure his job, forget that, his life would be on the line when he went back to work this time.

Jimmy packed the money in his shoe box with the rest and attempted to go to sleep but his mind kept going back to the days in that jail cell. All he could smell was shit and lotion, everything nasty about that place was running through his every thought. He would rather be dead than to do a longer bid in that hell hole. He was pondering on all the places they could send him depending on the charges they chump up on him.

Jimmy was getting scared to death, he couldn't eat and was damn near about to throw up the little bit of food he ate earlier. He took 2 Benadryls and was out like a light 15 minutes later.

Straight into his dreams, Jimmy had a new whip, a new crib and was even dating one of his Instagram crushes he was drooling over named Dominique. Spending money was a habit and he stayed in all designer everything. Debbie was a maid that cleaned his condo and Willow was his blunt roller. Eric was his Shofer that only could talk when spoken to. Mr Figaroa where are we off to today, shut up I didn't say you could speak. Jimmy was laughing in his sleep. He ran his own security company, it's like he turned that little money he was blessed with by God of course into multi-millions overnight.

Jimmy was set and didn't want to wake up out of his fantasy land where everything was perfect and real. He brought his mother her dream house and his father an F150 truck in silver he always asked him for. Life was good in his dream world,never having a rainy day.

8

Debbie was busy all day at the Hospital, she was working a double trying to put this money together for the trip with her Boo. Mr Gibson was sent home a couple of days ago so her little play money was gone. She was in her Bosses office checking his schedule to see what was he lining up before she went away on vacation. Couple of new clients and a home visit was all he had on his agenda, nothing that needed her special attention. So she watered his plants and fed his goldfish, Bluto from the movie Popeye. He always ordered her to do that when he went home early for the day to spend time with his family.

As Debbie went to lock up his office and step out to check her patients on the floor for the night she was pushed back into the office by none other than Crystal conniving ass.

There you go, said Crystal with her hand popping Debbies bottom like they've been best friends for years.

O hi, whats up, why are you stalking me now all of a

sudden, said Debbie confused from all this attention Crystal has been giving her lately. You don't have work to do? I heard you've been looking for me. How can I help you, do you need some advice on a patient or something?

Nope, I need you on this floor butt naked, now strip I got ten minutes to spare that's

All I need to pop that cherry of yours real good too.

Debbie was taken back, Crystal was being really aggressive lately that's why she was trying to stay clear of her.

Listen lady Im strictly Dickly and I dont know what you heard but you need to calm the fuck down before this goes left real good too. Now back up and get out of my Bosses office before I make a mess with you up in here, Debbie was starting to get annoyed.

Nuh, relax I think you're so cute, I just wanted to confirm our date night. I got a spot in the Bronx called Evo we could meet at. Good food, music and drinks. I'm trying to be your friend, that's all. I swing but if you ain't like that I totally understand. I got a date ready and everything, we can go out this wednesday night I know you're off and I took off so what's up, let's let our hair down and get right with ya girl one time before you go on your little vaca.

You know a lot about me, said Debbie, questioning this hangout night to herself. She knows Crystal from work but she really dont know her, know her, you know. They never had more than lunch talk in the cafeteria and even that was getting extra spicy, touchy- feely. She damn near was touching her privates under the table rubbing Debbie thighs in a close conversation about what type of lingerie they buy and how things fit their voluptuous bodies.

She wasn't scared of Crystal because she could handle herself with the hands, and had been fighting since young. Debbie had her share of problems coming up, her and her sister fighting the whole block, people being jealous because all the guys wanted them, it was a trip and she got the battle scars to prove it.

Ight, said Debbie we lit Im down. Now step out of this office before people get too inconspicuous about us.

Crystal was hype and she let Debbie go to continue her night. Quick give me your number and imma text you mine, said Crystal as she popped Debbie's ass to see it wiggle one last time.

I'll see y'all later!

Imma beat you up, keep your paws to yourself before I, she popped Crystal back on her bottom and the wave was crazy.

Ya, you ain't never felt a pillow softer than mine, trust me said Crystal.

Debbie was moved; she couldn't lie, it was real too.

Crystal walked away with a hard switch and a slutty look back like Debbie could get it any time she was ready.

What I'm getting myself into she thought as she began her bed check. Thank God Jimmy was going to be there with her so she wasn't worried about the date.

Her phone vibrated and Crystal texted her, hit me anytime!

Debbie shook her head and stored the number. I got

you wednesday night imma hit you around 6 o'clock we could meet by 8 because I have to work the next morning.

That's all the time I need. Crystal texted back with a heart and happy face.

This Bitch so skimmy, Debbie thought to herself. I gotta watch her, she's trying to get you Shadicka. The name she gave her kitty cat back in the day when she was in them streets.

Debbie finished her run then went to the break room hoping that's the last she saw of Crystal for the night. She called Jimmy but he didn't answer so she texted him her love. Telling him about the date and how she couldn't wait to get that slung on the beach. She knew that would make him hit her back when he woke up and saw the message.

Debbie was so tired she started to daydream about her high school days in the Bronx. Debbie went to Our Lady of Refuge an all girl Catholic school so this wasn't her first rodeo with a female coming on to her. She had a couple occasions where she teased the idea of being with a woman. It even happened a few times with her girlfriend Patrica. Patrica was a beautiful hispanic hot momma, fresh from Puerto Rico and she was coming with the smoke. Catching Debbie in the bathroom, one time in the staircase. She didn't know what they was feeding Patica in her Arroz Con Gandules but she was strong as fuck. Debbie tried to fight her off but she was so promiscuous that she just had to let her have it. They played off and on for damn near 2 years until Debbie took the star of the basketball team from Saint Raymonds all boys Catholic school Benjamin to the prom. Patricia wasn't crushed but that was then the end of that when Benjamin aka (Bentley) the name they gave him because he looked like money and played so silky on the courts.

Bentley put the slam dunk on Debbies little ass that night. They started dating after graduation and Patrica moved to Florida with her family, last Debbie heard from her cousin that was still good friends with her. She wasn't made at the experience though that was her childhood and her past and she loved it all. Made her the woman she was today.

Debbie was guessing that's what Crystal was sensing in her. They say real recognize real so Crystal must sense that Debbie could swing with the right influences. She hasn't played like that in years, she's in a loving relationship with Jimmy and that is that.

9

Jimmy woke up in a pool of water with the money box open thinking about everything that happened praying this situation wouldn't come back and bite him in his behind. The cameras are still out of commission so he has that on his side plus he hasn't told no one but how is this only happening when he's at work. No one has said anything funny yet about money being misplaced or stolen so for now he's in the clear he hopes.

He grabbed his phone and read Debbies text about the party. Maybe that's exactly what he needed a chill night to pop some bottles and drink. Have a blast with his baby before they go away, why not!

Jimmy started thinking smart, he had to invest that money just in case things got hot he couldn't get caught with that money on him so he decided to spend it just as fast as it came. If he goes to jail then he better enjoy himself before anything like that happens. He just hopes and prays that Debbie holds him down. Hopefully this trip will stamp their love and she stays with him forever. Jimmy is not too much into marriage but Debbie is definitely marriage material. She's bad, in her early 20s, no kids and has a great career going for herself. If he doesn't marry her someone will, especially if he has to do a hefty bid off this bank shit. So that got him thinking heavily on buying her a ring finally. It's been about 5 years and they never really talked about it. They moved like they were but nothing signed on the dotted line.

Jimmy got himself together and grabbed about 25,000 out the box and drove straight to Major world in Queens. He bounced before Debbie got home so he could surprise her. He had been looking at a 2019 Tahoe like the one he had but in way better shape going for 19,000 straight. Low mileage, fairly new, one owner and no accidents. All black with gray interior with a banging system, fully equipped with twenty inch chrome rims.

Jimmy had to have it, he took it for a test drive and fell in love. Truck ride was so smooth it felt like a Lincoln continental. Jimmy pulled the dealer to the side. Harvey, a young black fast talking hood guy in a suit and tie, just the person he needed to tweak that paper work and give him the keys today.

He showed Harvey the cash and told him to keep the whole 25 if he let the deal go through now. He took Jimmy to the waiting area, Debbie was blowing his phone up so he called her back while he waited.

Where the hell are you at? said Debbie worried because he always calls or text her back quickly.

Dont trip momma im doing something nice for us and I

need to talk to you about something serious when I get home. We're gonna grab some lunch before I go to work. Give me about an hour and I'll be outside to pick you up. You're gonna like this!

Debbie hung up the phone and jumped in the shower to freshen up and get dressed. She got real cute putting on an outfit that showed off all her assets in the right places. Played a little music and layed down on the couch because she was still a little tired from her double. As soon as she was about to go out completely her phone rang and Jimmy told her to come downstairs to the front of the building.

Debbie rinsed off her face and went down the stairs looking fine. Willow was in the staircase with his boys and they started whispering right away.

Dang you smell good Miss Debbie said Willow, Jimmy so lucky, you got a sister right?

Yeah but she is older than me, little boy. You're about my niece's age but you gotta get yourself together. All this weed smoking and gangster rapping I can't plug you into my family said Debbie.

I'm about to be the next big thing, said Willow as he walked Debbie to the door to see Jimmy pull up. In his new 2019 Tahoe on dubs.

Jimmy rolled down the window and told Willow to get his ass away from his wife.

O shit, said Willow escorting Debbie to the truck still holding her hand and waist like a young gentleman.

Jimmy hopped out looking like a NYC mack, pushed Willow to the side and opened the door for Debbie as he palmed her ass leaving Willow in the front of the building with his mouth open stuck.

Get your money up little fella, said Jimmy as he pulled off.

Willow threw him the bird and walked back into the building with his Goonies

Debbie started right away with a thousand questions. Whose truck is this? How'd you get the money? And what did you do to get it?

It's our truck, I saved up and traded in mine for a 2,500 down payment and I only have to pay 250 a month on the deal I got so just enjoy the ride baby. Lying through his teeth Jimmy felt great to be on the high end of the stick for once.

Debbie looked so good he wanted to pull over and get busy in the backseat real quick to break the truck in. He probably would have tried it if it wasn't 12 o'clock in the afternoon and he wasnt so damn hungry.

Where are you taking me said Debbie, hungry herself looking around the truck admiring the new car smell and the way her ass felt on the gray leather seats.

We are going to the Lighthouse in Harlem, I'm starving and I want a good drink to celebrate the new whip.

Lighthouse is a great soul food spot on 116th street and the east side. Always popping any time of the day. They usually have a DJ playing the latest tunes with TVs in the back playing the latest sports event for the day. Best of both worlds, music for Debbie and sports for Jimmy.

Jimmy ordered the sweet chicken and shrimp platter with collard greens and mac & cheese., Debbie ordered the fried flounder and shrimp with yams and potato salad because Jimmy ordered her other favorite sides they usually share with each other because the sides are so colossal it's enough to eat and take food home.

Give me 2 waters and I would like a Nut cracker and a Long Island for my lady said Jimmy as he glanced at the basketball game that was about to start wishing he could go home with his woman but he had to drop her home and go to work, not because he wanted to because he had enough accumulated time to call out. He just wanted to go in and face the music once again to see if the coast was clear and he didn't have to go to jail for 10 or 15 years.

He grabbed Debbie's hands waiting for the food, looked into her eyes just to see how she felt about him without using any words. He could tell she was deeply in love, they both were then he asked her. What do you think about marrying ya boy?

Debbie almost spit up her water as she blushed with glee. I knew you were going to say something like that when you said you wanted to talk said Debbie.

I feel like we're already married and a piece of paper might mess that up. I love what we got and sometimes when you get married things get worse and not better. Besides you gotta tell me your long term goals and what our future is going to look like before I say yes and grow old with you, you see I'm still a young fine tenderoni and I have to keep my options open for that baller to sweep me off my feet and fulfill all my dreams. I mean I'm just being honest my mother didn't raise a housewife. She taught me to be independent and reach for the stars so as my husband you may have to step your game up. Are you ready for that?

Debbie wasn't holding any punches, Jimmy didn't know whether to get upset or step up to the plate and hit a homerun. She obviously is not ready to settle where she is at in life and she wants a lot more so he had to get his shit together. He's living a check to check life and if it wasn't for Debbie's income he would be struggling on his own so he had a lot to think about before he could even talk about a marriage with her.

The food came and Jimmy got real quite obviously not really hearing what he wanted to hear from his lady.

Debbie cleaned it up before things went left, look baby i'm not going anywhere I just know we could do better. Get a house, have a nice bank account and some insurance before we start talking about kids and marriage. We are still trying to have fun with one another. This is our first big trip together and we've been together for almost 5 years. I want to see the world a little before I get locked down but yes I will definitely marry you when the time is right. Ok!

Okay said Jimmy holding his face in his plate trying not to give her any eye contact.

Debbie lifted up his head and gave him a soft kiss so he could smile again.

She knew what to do to butter him up. This aint about us, this about you and your new beautiful truck parked out front. That's a great start baby got your girl riding in style. That old Tahoe was sweatpants and air ones, this one is minks and gator shoes.

Jimmy started laughing, his mind was racing on what

he had to do to make this woman feel secure but he wasn't discouraged. He was really glad they had this talk. It was sort of clarity for him to figure his life out and step his game up. He knew Debbie wasn't a woman to be held just by a dick game. He had to be hitting on all cylinders to keep her or Mr Right was going to come in and take her right from under him for sure.

They Finished eating, Debbie noticed Jimmy left a substantial amount of money for a tip. They jumped back in the truck and she jumped into him giving him a thousand kisses to thank him for the date. Jimmy wasn't moved; he knew she was dying to get that conversation off her chest. They've been working so hard coming and going for so long he really didn't know how his lady felt about him deep down inside. He had some changes to make quick and fast.

He dropped Debbie off at home nice and wet, Letting her know he's not going anywhere any time soon. She was stuck with him for life and he loved her dearly.

Jimmy proceeded to work not really worrying about the ATM money anymore and had bigger fish to fry, like going back to school and finding a better paying job so he wouldn't be working for Effective Security Company for long.

Eric walked straight to him before he could go in the back to change his clothes.

What the deal my boy? Ready for tonight, said Eric sarcastically.

Look out, said Jimmy, still a little piturved about his

date with his baby. Not even trying to tell Eric big mouth ass about his new truck or nothing.

Dang man what crawled up your ass and died I was just tryna check in with you.

Not today said Jimmy not really in the mood for chit-chat I'll holla at you later you could bounce and get your daughter. Tell her uncle Jimbo said hi.

Ight playboy. I'm gonna have a good shift and tell Debbie when she leaves you, get my number out your phone first.

Jokes, jokes she don't want another security guard so save the BS and get the fuck out my face.

Eric felt the tension flaring up so he didn't say another word he just grabbed his belongings and dipped.

Miss Helen was elated too; she was dancing by the water machine in the back and talking on the phone with her new Boo, Harold. She's not even trying to keep it on the low. She cant let people know she fucking one of the security guards thats still recognized as bank staff.

Jimmy just changed into his uniform and got to work. Break time he didn't even go for his smoke break. He just grabbed his phone and started looking for trade schools from computer tech to refrigeration, his eyes even went to real-estate. Real-Estate training course, free hands on out in the field training for one month. We'll teach you how to buy properties, no money down. If you want to get into the world of flipping houses for a profit join us for an orienta-tion every 15th and 23rd of each month.

Jimmy saved the number in his phone and highlighted the

orientation dates in his phone. He was really interested in that real-estate move. He put it number one on his agenda for the success of his future. He knows if he puts 110 percent into this he could be a great real-estate agent. Debbie put a real battery in his back and a fire up under his ass to do better for her. Jimmy even laughed because this is what he may have needed to be great. His mother and father always told him that Debbie was perfect for him and she could set him straight in life so they were very happy she came into their son's life.

Jimmy had a plan to move forward and it felt great. The night went by fast and it was almost closing time. Jimmy was cleaning up before he locked up. The last person came in a rush to catch the doors before closing. As soon as Jimmy escorted him out and turned around the ATMs started right away.

Jimmy just sat on the windowsill and let the machines go. All 4 of them were ringing this time. Jimmy was just going to walk out and leave the money on the ground and quit. He really didnt know what to do at this point. It took him 15 minutes to get all the cash up off the floor after the machines went back to normal. He stuffed all the money in his work bag which was a lot. Everything was going in slow motion. Jimmy locked up slowly and went to his truck slowly, drove home slowly and sat in the Tahoe for an hour and a half before he texted Debbie he was home.

Jimmy went upstairs and threw his work bag on the coach. Jumped in the shower to wash off his guilt, Then he dried off, sat next to the bag and stared at it in disbelief. He had to go to the store and get a six pack of Modelo Negro to figure all this shit out. He drank 2 then started to count the money. Took him 2 hours to count 100,000 which left him flabbergasted. He neatly stacked all the cash in his shoe box and slid it back under his side of the bed. Thank God Debbie never goes through his shoe boxes because he has so many. Jimmy buys 2 pairs of sneakers every month but he doesn't hoarder, he gives the ones he doesn't wear to the salvation army before he piles up too many around the crib. He wouldn't even know how to begin to explain that money to Debbie. He really doesn't know how she would take it if she found out. Debbie could be heard to deal with at times so it's best he tells no one unless he's forced to.

Debbie has been working the night shift for the last couple of days so she was so ready to punch out and get some sleep but it's party night with Miss Crystal so she wants to rest up to have the energy to beat a bitch ass tonight if need be.

Debbie ran to the train and caught the express uptown bound to get home as quickly as possible. Time moves fast when you make plans to go out.

Finally home she was kinda exhausted. Jimmy was still knocked out on the couch in the living room. Debbie thought he looked so sweet when he's asleep so she quietly straightened up his mess, turned off the television, jumped in the shower and hit the bed like a branch falling off a tree after a bad storm.

10

Jimmy was the first to resurrect from the dead. He saw his baby cleaned up after him so he decided to run out and get some breakfast from Mcdonlds for them before she came too.

Ran past the door man Willow as he smacked him on his head to keep him in line.

Yo bro said Willow, watch the due, where are you off to now? Let me hold your truck so I can spend the block for some booty.

Umm Hell no, going to get some Mickey Ds said Jimmy in a rush. You want something?

Bring me back an egg Mcmuffin I'm starving you right on time said Willow, holding his stomach like he hadn't eaten in weeks.

Walking to Mcdonalds not wanting to move the truck because he caught the right side last night with the alternate parking. Going into the restaurant he heard his name being called, Jimmy!

What up Jr what going on buddy boy?

Nothing much, getting some breakfast for the clan my moms ain't feel like cooking this morning so I gotta spend like 100 dollars to feed everyone today so you know I'm tight, right!

How's everything with you, you were pretty stressed the other day. Did you settle your situation?

Nuh you know how it is, more money, more problems. Just gotta be smart and stay ahead of the game, said Jimmy as he ordered.

Let me get 2 bacon egg & cheese biscuits, 2 sausage ones and an egg Mcmuffin separately please.

Jr ordered like the same times 10 with 3 coffees and 3 orange juices.

Dang said Jimmy, you straight I'm going to head back to the block, imma definitely catch you later stay up!

Easy said Jr asking for more bags so he can package his food better so he dont drop anything.

Jimmy hit the block and Willow was sitting on the steps listening to his little demo he made in the studio the other day.

You listen to your boy, Willow said as Jimmy gave him his sandwich.

The beat was hard and Willow was going off as usual. Jimmy heard him spit in the hallway a couple of times and he wasn't bad. Willow sounded like a young Styles P, hard NYC flow with his own twisted flavor with like Waka Flocka ad libs. Hook was dope, beat was street, Jimmy felt like it could play in the clubs a definite radio banger, Flex would drop 2-3 bombs for sure. Took him back he listened to 2 tracks before he went upstairs to feed his baby.

Debbie woke up as Jimmy was making coffee in the kitchen. She went to pee after giving him a hot mouth morning kiss.

Hey baby I got you some breakfast and started the coffee said Jimmy looking at her booty jiggle to the kitchen table to eat.

Yo you gotta hear Willow new tracks they are fire I can't even hold you. He sounds 10 times better then these new rappers in the game.

I think Willow wants me to hear something else, Debbie started laughing with her head back.

Jimmy didn't find that funny at all with his overprotective self. Eat your breakfast before you make me end his career before it starts. But not for nothing on a serious note he got it forreal with the right team he can definitely go from crib to palace in a few years. Imma talk to him about performances. We're gonna pop out for him to show him some support, I mean we knew him since he was 13.

I'm with that said Debbie finishing up her food heading back to the bed with Jimmy on her heels to get some more sleep.

You're ready to party tonight, we're going in said Jimmy. Imma make sure we have a great time. Got the new whip, I'm getting super fly and I'm chilling with my best girl, tonight.

I'm ready, I want to dance tonight said Debbie I hope the music is good. I]\ never been to EVO Lounge. Crystal crazy ass bringing a date so you gonna have to play nice. I hope he's not a male her I don't know if I could take 2 Crystals.

Jimmy kissed Debbie all over her face, I got you as they went back to slumberland.

11

Debbie was the first up refreshed, since she takes the most time she jumped in the shower first to get herself together. She pulled out her freak him dress because she plans to wear no panties because Jimmy was gonna have her tonight any time any place. She checked her phone to like 3 texts from Crystal and 1 missed call. She called back just to make sure everything was still a go.

Crystal sounded like she was getting worked over in the background when she answered the phone. Um what are you doing? said Debbie not knowing what to expect from this woman.

I'm getting a massage. I like to get stretched out with all them hours at the job I try to go every other week. That's what I was calling and texting you for a little pampering for my girl before we get busy tonight on the dance floor. If you want to get your nails done, that's my next stop. I can come scoop you. I got a couple of nips so we can start this party early.

That doesn't sound like a bad idea. I could tell Jimmy to come pick me up, then come back and get dressed. Let me throw a sweatsuit on and imma text you my address. I could use some acrylic and a fresh paint job on these nails asap.

I'll be done here in 10 minutes, my nail salon is on Westchester Square and I live on Castle Hill. If you want to come get dressed by me bring your stuff we could get ready together. Jimmy will be fine he could meet us there. I'll tell my date the same, Evo is by Park Chester near my crib. I go there all the time, Crystal said, everybody knows me.

I'm sure Debbie said to herself, she told Jimmy the plan who was half asleep. He was fine meeting her there as long as she was ok with it he was.

By the time Debbie put her sneakers on Crystal was downstairs. Debbie grabbed her bags with her purse, dress and shoes so she could get dolled up and blow Jimmy's mind tonight.

Crystal was outside blasting Trey Songz album, cleaning her sunglasses in her 2023 KIa Forte all red looking real cute and being harassed by none other than Willow.

Miss Debbie who is this, can I have this one said Willow as she got in the car on the passenger side.

Boy go find you something to do said Debbie laughing as Crystal leaned over and gave her a seductive kiss on her lips.

Hey girl said Crystal before Debbie could say something about that greeting kiss.

Dang said Willow as he fixed his glasses and leaned into the window so he could have one too.

Back up, said Debbie, let's go girl before he jumps in the back seat and rides around with us all day and we can't get rid of him.

Where yall going said Willow ready to go too.

To get our nails done, you need your nails done said Crystal making a guy juster.

Hell nuh said Willow but you could give me your number so I can call you later to see what's up

See what's up with what little boy, maybe in a couple of years and a lot of more digits I can let you call me. To hear my voice on the phone, you're not near ready for this ride.

You don't know what I can do said Willow as the ladies laughed and pulled off leaving Willow in the rear view looking sad as he could be.

Imma be that guy Willow yelled as he threw them the bird and walked to the store to get him some munchies he was higher than a mug and that egg Mcmuffin been worn off hours ago.

Don't pay his little ass no mind his mother should have sent him away years ago. All he does is play this tired ass block and harass people that walk in and out. I'm about to tell Jimmy to give him a job doing security because he can post up for hours. Wannabe rapping ass, I'm so ready to move it's a shame, said Debbie looking in the sun visor mirror at her pretty face.

Love yo car girl this is nice, Jimmy just got us a new Tahoe. It's comfortable as hell, I got my license but I hate to drive in New York. This traffic is outta hand, the trains move faster than the vehicles, all the tickets and construction, if Jimmy doesn't drive me I just Uber if I ain't going to the job.

Well I love to drive, I be moving, I just hate to let people control my time, I be out. I have a daughter but she stay in Atlanta with her father. We didn't work out and he didn't want another man around his baby. So I live by myself and she comes up here every summer but this summer we decided to do camp so I'm just working and chilling. He got me on child support now ain't that a bitch. That's why I was doing all them hours, Bitch got bills like a mug. But I keep it sexy though as you can see.

Crystal popped her ass, put the music up and handed Debbie a snip of Casamigos. I got you an ice cup and cranberry or orange juice in the bag.

A woman after my own heart said Debbie.

I'm tryna tell you I got you Boo, now let's get these nails done, get real cute and see how the night plays out, cause you can get it if you want it, i'm just saying. I'm ready when you are, she grabbed Debbie's thigh and looked at her with real seriousness in her actions.

You need to stop, Debbie said, you are too much, this gonna be a long night I can tell already.

Crystal put on her shades and let it go for now. Debbie started talking about nail colors as they boogied to the nail salon.

She wasn't worried about Crystal's attempts; she always acted like that since the day they met. If Crystal goes too far Debbie has no problem checking the situation. This has been going on for three plus years even though this is the first time they've hung out. Everything has been work related but Debbie didn't have many girl friends since High School, just her family so she's ready for the shits tonight. Been a minute so Crystal can say what she wants all her true girlfriends acted the same way so she was used to being attacked. Shit she would attack herself if she was in their shoes. That's how bad she is,.everybody has wanted her since she was a kid, men and women.

Nail salon was packed but Crystal had her appointment set up. These 2 ladies are the best. This is Ming and this is Kio. I've been coming here for 3 years. They used to be near Simpson now they moved closer to me and I love it.

As the girls sat down to pick their colors Crystal cell rang.

Hey Boo. Yes, I'm at the nail salon now with my friend. We're going to be poppin, you got that thing for me, Ok then meet us at EVO by 8:30, hit me and I'll come out to get you, tonight gone be crazy. The turn up is real, SMOOCHIES!

That's my little Boo Boo Marvin, he is definitely a turn up. I can't wait for you to meet him.

How long y'all been dating? said Debbie, curious because she only heard Crystal talk about women. This is even her first time hearing about a baby daddy and a daughter.

We were down for forever we almost like family said Crystal getting her nails filed down, ooch watch that Ming, you messing up your tip already.

They made some more drinks because they had to do their toes too.

Crystal couldn't take her eyes off Debbie, but she stayed in line.

You picked some nice summer colors said Crystal as she watched Kio create an ocean design on Debbie's nails. She put the ocean blue, yellow and white. All white on the toes, looking real cute.

Crystal got her french tips on, fingers and toes, grown and sexy style.

We are definitely ready for the night, Jimmy's mouth is gonna be on the floor when he sees me. Debbie was admiring herself in the mirror before they bounced to Crystal's crib.

Crystal lived like literally 4 blocks away, she had the first floor of an all private house with a drive in right off Castle Hill. The girls went in and Debbie was moved by how clean it was. Crystal had a little style you could tell she had some major coordination, Her color scheme matched threw the whole front, nice big furniture. She took her time. Debbie checked out the whole place as she rushed to the bathroom. She didn't have to go in the salon.

Debbie came out of the bathroom with more compliments.

Crystal went in the kitchen and made more drinks, Debbie joined her and they both just started talking about work and family real quick.

Look at the time said Crystal, I'm about to jump in the shower real quick, you're always welcomed to join me if you want. She started getting undressed intentionally in front of Debbie, then she turned showing her bare bottom and went into the bathroom.

Debbie, no thank you, I'm just gonna get dressed out here.

As the shower started Debbie went for her bags and pulled out her easy access bang um dress. All she had on her mind was Jimmy as she texted him, i'm getting dressed now, we're gonna meet you at EVO. Her date name is Marvin, 8 o'clock be there I want to see u with you handsome self.

Text me a picture of what you put on, I'm getting dressed now. I can't wait to see you.

Debbie took her clothes off down to the thong. She slipped her curvy body into a tight fitting summer yellow dress that zipped down top to bottom from the side. Then she pulled out some black Chanel Mesh ankle strapped sandals. Chanel Clutch with Black Chanel shades that matched looking super sexy. She leaned back on Crystal Coach and caught a shot of her whole ensemble, Send!

Crystal came out of the bathroom wrapped in a towel, she froze when she saw what Debbie put together. Okay Diva!

Imma have to go deep in my bag to catch up to you.

Real deep said Debbie as she sprayed herself with a bottle of Chanel Chance. You finished in the bathroom little girl. I just want to take a look and freshen up my make-up and hair. I'll be 3 minutes tops so get dressed. I'm already ready.

Oh I see everything said Crystal damn near drooling

over her as she watched her switch that thing into her bath-room, You need any help?

I'm good, drink is hitting and I'm ready to ride my man all night long.

Crystal rolled her eyes, sucked her teeth and continued to dry off walking towards her bedroom. She saw all her attempts were falling short. She knew she was going to need to get Debbie drunk to get her mind off wanting Jimmy. But the night was still young and she didn't want to make Debbie uncomfortable, she wouldn't want to come back if she did. So she played her cards right, turned some music on and put on her own freak him dress looking hella succulent her damn self.

Marvin's gonna be all over you said Debbie, Crystal laughed and put on her Versace Bright Crystal. Of course she brought it because of her name, why not!

We ready , they yelled as they walked out the door to EVO.

Jimmy was going crazy off her picture. He called her 3 times before she made it to the Lounge

Crystal was turning up the radio every time it rang trying to be funny.

Debbie didn't pay her no mind.

12

Jimmy pulled up next to Crystal's car with his big ass Tahoe. Crystal told him where to park as the girls parked and waited for him to walk over to the car to greet them. When he saw his baby step out he straight molested her with affection.

You look so damn good, you sure you want to go inside. We gots to bless the truck, his interest was making Debbie blush from ear to ear.

Crystal cleared her throat, yall ready.

O hi shorty, I'm sorry as Jimmy greeted Crystal with a kind hug and smooch. Nice to finally meet you, heard a lot of nice things, lying out his teeth.

They all proceeded to go inside EVO.

The bouncers checked Jimmy Thoroughly, and checked the girls purses for liquor and drugs.

The lights in the lounge were flashing like they stepped into a video. The waitress escorted them to a table of four near the back by the kitchen. There they could see everyone coming in. Everyone knew Crystal so they didn't even ask her what she was drinking. Before Debbie could even say his name, Marvin stepped through the crowd looking quote the davineer himself. Crystal greeted him with a hug and introduced him as they all sat down at the table.

The DJ was on a High stage rocking the latest hits. He threw on Kendrick, they not like us and everyone started to cheer and boogie in the middle of the floor set for dancing.

Jimmy called over the waitress girl who was damn near naked and asked for bottle service. That's what I'm talking about, said Crystal as Debbie was looking in awe.

We good, Jimmy whispered to her as she let him rock with no embarrassment.

Let me get 2 bottles of Don Julio dark and some Hookah, cranberry juice, ice and orange juice.

I got the bottles but I'll send the Hookah guy your way said the waitress looking at Jimmy like a snack. Debbie was getting defensive, ight don't start nothing, won't be nothing letting the bottle girl know that her man is taken.

Marvin yelled out, I got the food as he raised his hand like he was still in middle school. I'm starving, and have been working for 2 days straight in Brooklyn.

What do you do, said Jimmy?

Construction, I've been doing it for about 3 years now. Working on 2 different sights right now but I'm here and we're gonna get lit tonight.

Give me 2 sample trays with mozzarella sticks, artichoke dip, chips and buffalo wings with ranch dipping sauce. Yall want anything, said Mavin as they all laughed.

A group of ladies came through the crowd with the beverages and the sparkles on the bottles. As the Hookah guy set up his pipe and asked them what flavor they liked. Crystal was ecstatic about the mint so everyone went with that.

They all made drinks and cheered to a new found friendship. Half of the first bottle was done by the time the food came. Everyone was having a good time, Jimmy was telling Marvin about his security career and the real-estate moves he's about to make.

Debbie was telling Crystal about all the stuff she brought for the Mexico trip. The DJ put on some Old school R&B and Crystal pulled Debbie to the floor to dance. That's my shit, ready or not, you can't hide, here I come, gonna find you and take it slowly. The Fugees was her favorite album when she was younger. She started to grind on Debbie like they were dry humping. Jimmy started to take a little notice but Marvin was playing defiance and distracted him by talking about one of the bottle girls that looked like Rihanna, same big head and everything.

When Jimmy finally looked back again they were coming back to the table for another round of drinks. Everyone stopped and turned to Marvin who was devouring them platters. Thank God they all made a nice plate when it arrived.

Jimmy pulled Debbie to the side to get his rub on, just to let her know he's trying to devour something too.

That was all the time Crystal needed to get Marvin to finally use that thing she asked him to bring. He reached over and dropped a powdery substance in Debbies drink. Just as fast as Debbie turned around Crystal gave her her cup and cheered to a bomb night. She then took her whole drink to the head and dared Debbie to do the same. She did as Marvin started grinning at Crystal like it was a mission complete.

20 minutes later Debbie wasn't feeling too good, so she decided to drink some water which forced her to go to the bathroom. Crystal joined her, taking their purses to straighten up. Jimmy was having such a blast with Marvin he ended up ordering a bottle of Blue Bellaire. He wanted to still party but cut off the heat from more hard liquor. Marvin didn't care about anything; he was full and ready to go all night. He asked Jimmy what beer he fucked with, Modelo Negro Jimmy uttered as Marvin went to the bar to get a bucket.

Crystal was in the bathroom Helping Debbie damn near throw up. Then she noticed they were finally alone. This was her opportunity to take Debbie in her weekend state.

Now I got you, you know I wanted you for so long. She pushed Debbie into a stall, locked the door and attacked her like a tiger going for his prey. Debbie was so weak all she could do was hold on to the arm bar and brace herself for contact so she did not hit the floor. Crystal took her fingers and spelled the whole alphabet in Debbies box. They were in there for 15 minutes. Jimmy was about to check on them until he saw Debbie coming towards him looking drunker than a mother. She sat on his lap as Crystal gave him Debbies purse.

Somebody twisted Marvin said as Jimmy was asking her if she was ready to go.

Crystal said imma get her some more water. Give her these Benadryls I got in my bag and she'll be brand new in the morning, no hangover at all.

Jimmy finished off his bottle kinda tight as he escorted his baby out the party. He didn't even get a chance to dance and put his moves on her. Crystal helped them as Marvin stayed inside drinking his beers.

Crystal came back inside and cracked one with him, Thanks cuzzo I got her good. She's mine, had her screaming for her life in there. She doesn't know about that roofy game, said Marvin. You line 'em up and I'll knock' em down. All day as Marvin chuckled, Crystal zeroed in on another victim by the bar and Marvin sat at another table with some ladies that were eyeing him the whole time. What took you so long? I had to help my cousin handle her business. No time like the present, what are y'all getting into tonight?. Hopefully you, said the boldest one in the bunch. Marvin was flattered then he called Crystal over so everyone could get acquainted and goto her crib for a nightcap.

Jimmy was driving home with the AC on high so Debbie wouldn't throw up in his new ride.

You ok baby? We didn't drink like that in a while, you had fun?

Jimmy was rambling while Debbie was trying to hold it together.

I'm twisted but I'll survive, I don't know how I got hit so fast you made my drinks strong man. Did I eat? asked

Debbie as she told Jimmy to pull over and park. She jumped out the truck and vomited all over the sidewalk. As she got back in and cracked another water to drink Crystal flashed across her mind like a speeding camera. Imma get her ass Debbie uttered to herself trying to keep her head up.

What did you say momma?

The pills were kicking in and she was starting to think clear again.

Nothing, how was your night? My handsome man.

It was nice but I didn't get to get my groove on with you like Crystal did. She's a beast like you said, gotta watch her ass, said Jimmy.

Debbie looked into his eyes and climbed in the back of the truck hitting Jimmy with her backside to let him know he could get his dessert.

Jimmy smacked her on her butt and followed her like a og in heat. Debbie was still weak so she just laid back and opened her legs to let Jimmy get what he was longing for all day. I dont have my condemns, we gotta hit up a store. Debbie covered his mouth and whispered in his ear fuck the store.

Jimmy went to town taking full advantage of the situation. He was searching for some paper towels that he could release and Debbie got strength outta nowhere. She locked on him as his children went on that journey up to the creek.

When they were done he just kept looking at Debbie like she was crazy. Like she was about to disappear into a mist and be gone forever. Marriage kept popping up in his mind as he continued to drive home. She made him forget about all his problems, his job on the line, the money. He really was head over heels for this woman and he knew he had to get his life together to keep her.

Debbie was done, Jimmy carried her upstairs and put her into the shower. He was a complete gentleman, he made her some soup, coffee and a butter bagel so she wouldn't go to bed with an empty stomach.

Before she went down she texted her Boss and told him she would be coming in for the evening shift only, something major came up and she had to take off this morning. The way she felt she was going to need a little more sleep especially after having a double dose of fun. She knew exactly what Crystal did, how she was going to handle it was another question all together. She let her guards all the way down, Jimmy didn't catch on so it was cool. Paybacks a mother, but she didn't know if she wanted to set her up or beat her up. She had to play this one smart. Crystal knows where she works and lives. Strategic moves only, Jimmy grabbed her phone and pulled her in the bed. He wrapped her up with his big arms and made her go to sleep.

Come on baby, tomorrow's another day it's bedtime, hit that light.

I love you, good night!

13

Jimmy woke up and let Debbie get some well needed rest after the night she had. He grabbed 20 thousand out of the sneaker box and decided to do a little splurging for himself. He went to The Palisades Mall to hit up some stores real quick before work. Copped some jeans, a couple thin sweaters but he noticed he kept walking past Zales Jewelry store. Debbie was on his mind and the trip would be a perfect place to pop the big question. I think it's WEDDING RING time as he nervously walked over to there display of rings he heard,

Let me know if you need any help. You look like you got hit by the love bug, interested in any wedding rings the jeweler asked curiously.

Yes, I think it's definitely time to Beyonce my bae. What are the prices on these right here?

The jeweler pulled out a beautiful display of rings pricing from 5 to 100 thousand dollar wedding rings.

How much are you trying to spend today?

Not to make her nervous Jimmy pulled a 10 thousand stack out his pocket and gave it to her.

What can I get for that?

Well without evening being moved the jeweler placed a ring in his hand with the biggest shine he ever seen in his life.

5, CT. T.W. Quad Princess-Cut Diamond Frame Multi-Row Three Piece Bridal Set in 14K White Gold.

This is it Jimmy thought to himself but he still tried to be smooth and check out a couple others.

Put that aside, I'm definitely interested in that one, said Jimmy ecstatic about her first choice.

I'll give it to you for 7, 995.00 $, bag it up right now with insurance of 1,600 $ if damaged we can replace and fix anything that goes wrong with your beautiful purchase.

She went into the others but Jimmy kept his eye on the prize.

You know what, keep that 10 stacks and bag up the first choice.

Right away Sir, she put the ring in a exquisite suede and leather box with a light inside so if it's dark and Jimmy pops the question, that thing is gonna glisten Deddie pants right off her body.

Of course he did not leave without getting him a nice chain with a cross and pinky ring that caused him to drop another 5 thousand. Not too overwhelming but got the job done. Noticeable without making anyone Jealous or want to rob him on sight, CALM!

He just about spent all the cash in his pocket, Then called Debbie to make sure she was up and ready for work.

She didn't call back but she texted him.

On the run to work now, I missed you this morning, call me later and have a great shift, I love you big time, mwahhh!

Jimmy jumped in his truck looking so fresh and so clean feeling good about his purchases. He went to work on a good note, even showed Eric some love by bringing him some lunch from Chili's. Miss Helen was happy to inform him that the camera system would be back up and running by Monday so she could let her hair down because she will be getting her eyes back to keep watch on this money and the armored guards could finally come and pick up the cash in the safe.

Thank you Jesus!

Jimmy was happy too, he could be in the clear of all this mess, leaving for his trip Saturday so when he comes back he is definitely going to jump on that real-estate course so he can change careers asap.

Night went smoothly, everything was like clock work. He damn near was talking to himself thanking the ATM Gods for the recent glitches that set him straight for a few weeks now. All he has to do is lock up and bounce.

As soon as that thought came and Jimmy let out the last customer.

BOOM!

Fireworks, the ATMs were going crazy again.

Jimmy damn near passed out, he started shaking and going into commotion. He frantically put all the cash in his bag locked up and got out of there like he was being chased by the Feds.

Finally home pushing past Willow sweating from head to toe like he just played in a basketball tournament. He locked all 3 locks on his door and looked out the window to see if he was being followed, but nothing happened the other times. Why is this happening to me, he questioned himself. I'm going down, they're gonna throw my black ass in jail and make me swallow the key.

He began to count the money as he got out of the shower, checking his phone and looking out the window every 10 minutes. Debbie called him but he couldn't talk to her right now. He even left the clothes and the jewelry in the back seat.

Pull yourself together Jim, you didn't do shit and you don't know shit, you ain't tell nobody so you're good. Nobody knows but you and them crazy ass ATM machines and they can't talk, but you're on the ATM cameras, Get ready forJail fool!

Jimmy talked to himself and counted out 100,000 $ again. What the hell I'm I going to do, Debbie gonna leave me, my Moms gonna kill me after my dad choke me to death and tell the cops where he buried me. First 48, this is gonna be the Last 48 if I don't figure this mess out. I'll just give the money back and plead insanity, Stupid, Stupid, STUPID!

Debbie had a plan to get back at Crystal who was texting her all day.

Call me we have to talk I just want to apologize, this went too far, I was drunk too, don't kill me. Can we talk at work today, PLEASE!

How do you apologize for rapping someone and probably drugging me too. Debbie was furious but knew what she was going to do as she thought real quick to herself to get her revenge because this was definitely personal and payback is a must that's the hood rules. You don't snitch, you just get back in the same manner you were played.

Fuck it, before going to work Debbie went to a sex store in manhattan. She searched for the biggest dildo they had in the place, veins popping out and it was thicker than Jimmy's arm.

The store owner was looking at her like you better be careful after he saw what she was purchasing. Debbie went to work and everyone was telling her that Crystal was looking for her to talk to. Debbie didn't pay them any mind. She just clocked in and talked to her Boss that's leaving for the night and got his instructions off the board for his patients that she had to either introduce herself to or check on.

Debbie went into his drug supply that she was in charge of and set up a syringe of Fentanyl, a light dose will just put you out for a few hours. She greased up that big piece of wood she brought and put everything in the bag by her Boss desk on the floor. She knew Crystal was going to track her down there. She even got a wheelchair to move her body around to put her in a bed on her floor until the drug wears off. Sure enough Crystal came knocking on the door. Debble opened it and let the girl start pleading her case.

. . .

DEBBIE INVITED her in and locked the door. This made Crystal nervous but she knew she wasn't going to kill her in her boss's office so she kept apologizing. Debbie said it's all good. I actually had a good time but I'm really busy so we have to pick this conversation up later.

Cool, so you're not mad, Crystal went to turn and unlock the door and Debbie stuck her in the back of the neck with the drug then pushed her on the long couch the doctor had to counsel his patients. She pulled out the Dildo as Crystal tried to fight back. Debbie pulled her scrub pants down and went to work on her with that thing covering her mouth as Crystal got weak as the Fentanyl started to take effect and her eyes started rolling in the back of her head.

Debbie beat up every hole the girl had till her arm started hurting. She bagged up her sex weapon and put Crystal's clothes back on leaving her bottom all wet with her juices like she pissed her pants. Put her in the wheelchair, cleaned up the office, covered Crystal with a sheet and a pillow like a patient and put her on a bed in one of the rooms just like she would do any other client she had that was asleep. She didn't care if Crystal woke up and got fired. She was going to be out for a couple of hours. Debbie finished her shift and Crystal was still out when she left for home laughing at her get back.

If any more smoke the next step is to fight and both of them lose their jobs. Crystal is not gonna want that especially after what she did.

14

Jimmy couldn't go to sleep, he had to go outside with Willow and smoke to ease his tension. Willow was like a little brother so he didn't curse him out for pushing him earlier, he just passed the blunt to the left realizing Jimmy was definitely going through some shit because he barely ever smoked with him. You good? said Willow, curious about what's going on with his boy.

Jimmy just looked at him and said it's always gonna be some bullshit going on with me man. Imma figure it out just do me a favor if anybody comes looking for me, hit me up asap!

I got you, say less!

I'm out, he got all the bags out the truck and gave Willow a 50 spot just because.

Good looking if I hear your name come out of anyone's mouth I got you. Definitely!

Good night Lil Candy Bar, Baby Spliff Star, MC Stoop Doggy Dog!

They both laughed so hard, Jimmy needed that laugh when he went back in the crib he put the money and bags up and took it down for the night. He knew Debbie would be home soon and she never bothered him when he was asleep. He didn't want her to feel his stress because a thousand questions would come right after and she has a way of getting the truth out of him and he wasn't ready to spill the beans.

He wanted to be the first man to take his money to his grave, Literally!

Debbie came home in silent mode, Jimmy was out like a light so she closed the room door so she wouldn't disturb him. She grabbed a big pot and boiled her sex toy then hid it from Jim because he wouldn't begin to understand the wars women go through, plus she wasn't about to throw it away, not after paying 110 dollars for the thing. Debbie sat on the couch and thought about the whole ordeal she just encountered with this crazy ass chick. She definitely didn't think trying to give a person a chance to get to know her would turn out like this. Unfortunately they still had to work in the same establishment, Debbie wasn't transferring anywhere and she was going to keep Crystal in arms reach at all times. If she tries to even sit too close to her in the cafeteria she is gonna carry her scissors on her just in case.

Debbie began to doze off, as her phone started vibrating. It was Crystal! The nerve of her to call me thought Debbie looking curious in the face. She checked on Jimmy then answered the call.

You are really insane to call me, before she could begin to curse her out she heard Crystal crying. Cut the tears, said Debbie im not about to fall for that shit, just say what you have to say and be done with it.

Crystal fixed her voice to talk, my apology was a real one, you didn't have to do me like that I would have let you if you asked me. I almost got fired if my girls didn't cover me and told my Boss I had an emergency phone call from my daughter and I had to go. He would have canned me. I hope this makes us even, I don't want no more smoke, I love you and I just had to have you!

Wait, wait, what are you talking about? You love me, said Debbie, really confused. Now I know you're insane, you can't just take people you say you love and rap them when you get them drunk. You sound stupid as hell, you know I have Jimmy and what about your Boo Marvin.

Marvin is my cousin. I lied to get you to go out with me. I knew you wouldn't come out without bringing Jimmy. I fucked up, but I don't want you to hate me. I really want to have a relationship with you, you're so fine, you turn me on every time I see you. I love you, keep Jimmy we could move on the low;

Debbie hung up the phone, I don't believe she is still trying to come on to me after all of this. I know my stuff is good but come on now, she thought to herself while looking in the mirror.

Crystal kept calling back.

Debbie texted her back. Stop calling my phone before I block you. Then her phone got like six text messages.

It was pictures of Crystal in the tub naked, exposing all her goodies with love hearts and kisses.

You turned this kitty out, I want you, think about it!

Debbie couldn't do anything but smile, she wasn't even mad anymore she was kinda flattered. Crystal was bad as hell, Jimmy doesn't know, they can act like close girlfriends.

She texted back OK, when I come back from Mexico I'll see how I feel, but calm your ass down.

If we get caught imma beat your ass.

Debbie threw her phone down shaking her head not believing what she just agreed to. She thought about hurting Jimmy and losing everything they created these last couple of years. Why do the craziest people latch on to me?

She put on Housewives, cracked a bottle of wine she had in the fridge, grabbed her some chips then passed out after she finished her first glass.

Jimmy came to, like a mummy waking up from decades of slumber. He called out for Debbie who was comatose on the edge of the couch. He woke her and told her to get in the bed. Sleeping on the couch wrong for hours will fuck your back all up so he saved her some pain and him some stress from having to rub vicks all over her when she starts crying about aching.

The Trip was Saturday. They had to be on the plane at 2: 45 in the afternoon. So that means they had to be at the airport at 11 in the morning to be 3 hours ahead of time to register and check-in their bags.

Jimmy called his job to call out for the night, he was really nervous to walk back in there he still couldn't believe he had over 200,000 cash in his sneaker box under the bed.

He prayed that God would make all this make sense when he got back from Mexico.

15

Jimmy stayed up all night packing, He even stuffed a couple of G's in his luggage, Then cooked some breakfast for his love. Pancakes and sausages with some raspberry tea. Debbie has been packed for days. He didn't have to stress about her being ready. Jimmy told her he was calling out of work to get some rest because he knew he had to shofar all the bags so Debbie wouldn't break a nail. He called Eric and told him to hold it down. He called his parents and told them he was coming back with a fiance. They were elated, they just thought Debbie was so perfect for him. Everything was going smoothly. He put the ring up in a secret spot and he felt confident and ready for this next chapter.

Woke Debbie up for her breakfast then he was laid back out. Debbie just enjoyed her whole plate and half of Jimmy's too. She went to put her phone on charge because she still had to do one more shift before her getaway. Crystal texted her to pick her up for work, although

Debbie was hesitant she still was tired enough to take the ride. Jimmy needed his rest so she agreed.

Debbie freshened up, kissed Jimmy and told him she was going to work, Crystal was coming to pick her up and she wanted to take the ride.

He said ight and let her bounce, but he had to piss like a mother. As he proceeded to go to the bathroom, something just happened to make him look out the window. Crystal pulled up and picked up Debbie without her work bag, all she had was this white shopping bag and her purse.

He didn't want to jump to conclusions, maybe she's going to work to pick up a few things and come right back. He just shook off the feeling and went back to bed.

When Jimmy woke Debbie was in the living room with a bottle of casamigos and sprite. Playing music and pulling her bags to the door. How was work you home early, Jimmy spat out, how Crystal doing?

You know she is crazy as hell Debbie kicked back at him, she is still at work. She went back after dropping me home. I had to make sure my patients were alright and grab a few things from my locker. But I'm so ready to go ain't you?

Hell yeah, he made him a drink and pulled all his bags to the door.

They just sat the rest of the night talking and getting right, by the time they got sleepy Jimmy had to call an Uber.

After like half an hour loading the bags they were off to JFK in Queens. Debbie was so happy and made Jimmy feel good he made the moves with his job. Shit maybe all worth it if this trip goes well.

The whole ordeal of getting through bag check and body scans went faster than a mug. They were already getting sandwiches and beer from the mini-stores around their waiting area. The flight looked like it was going according to schedule so they decided to lay on each other and take a quick nap.

Jimmy couldn't sleep, he just held his baby and admired her looking at Debbie's cream skin and dark brown hair, picturing them together with 2 kids, a dog. Him driving everyone on a family vacation downsouth to play with her sister's kids. Cooking Bbq's and playing in the pool, with cards and arguing about who got the stinkiest farts, laughing to himself. He really loved this woman. When I hit her with this ring, she gonna cry and pass out, Jimmy thought to himself as they called to board the plane by section.

Straight flight to Cancun Mexico here we go, Jimmy woke up Debbie and they boarded the plane. Couple of nips with a movie and they were landing. Catching a cab to the Hilton was nothing. Everyone knew English at the airport. Jimmy paid the cab and exchanged numbers so they could call him to return to the airport, dude was cool so they didn't mind spending money on him. Pulse he dealt with all the luggage so they were good.

16

The Resort was so beautiful Debbie couldn't stop taking pictures, the waiting area, the big ass bar, they had like 2 or 3 restaurants on the main floor to choose from, They registered in, got that room key, 411 and went straight to the bar to get a drink, then the bus boy escorted them to there room with all there bags. Jimmy hit him with a twenty and got his name, Carlos glad to make your acquaintance. Anything you guys need and I'm around, please don't hesitate to ask, I'm here for you, to help you enjoy your stay at the Hilton.

Jimmy closed the room door, turned and Debbie was already damn near naked running the Jacuzzi they had on the balcony of the room past the glass screen doors. Jimmy put the bags in the bedroom, King size bed, mini fridge, a bathroom with a stand up shower. The mirror had a TV in it and the news was talking about how hot the weather was going to be for the next week, 90 degrees with a thunderstorm on wednesday. After that it was smooth sailings and he planned to cherish every minute of it. Full bar, microwave, 42' inch Television in the living room with a loveseat. Every room had matching paintings on the wells, very grown and sexy, the colors even put you in a happy mood, bright orange, yellow, dark blue and brown. Was hitting when the sun came in bouncing off Debbies wet body in that hot water. Jimmy had no choice but to join her as they made passionate love

Debbie gave him his money's worth, then they decided to go get dinner from downstairs, the food smelled so good on the way in, it was a must they found out where that aroma was coming from. They grabbed some brochures from the room that gave them the whole layout of the resort.

La Marea was the first spot for the night, Jimmy ordered a steak and rice platter while Debbie got 3 fully loaded tacos with avocados, chicken and shrimp that was so crazy she took some to go back to their room. The sun was going down so they took a quick tour to set up the agenda for tomorrow in the morning. Everyone treated them so nice, They saw the three pools out back that lead straight to the beach. Jimmy was in awe, he saw like 2 or 3 different spots he could propose to his Queen.

It looked like the whole hotel was on the beach enjoying the sun set. They had a fire pit going a little further down by a big statue of a Sea Lion. It was a small Hut that had a bar giving out free mixed tequila drinks like they were samples. You could order appetizers and charge everything to your room. They posted there, watched the sun set and got faded bonding for real like they first met.

Jimmy couldn't keep his hands off Debbie. She was loving every minute of it. They grabbed hands and walked along the beach admiring the scenery soaking in all the beauty and fresh air. They sat on the sand and talked until Debbie had to use the bathroom. Jimmy escorted her back to the main lobby and waited by the door. He pulled the ring out his pocket and looked at it, the lights by the bathroom made it sparkle like a crystal ball. Jimmy couldn't wait to pop the question. That ring was burning a hole in his pocket. He wanted to see it on Debbies finger already.

Debbie was in the bathroom admiring herself in the mirror and looking at her pictures she took of her and Jimmy. She definitely could see herself with him for a long time but he had to step up big time from that security guard shit. She always thought she would have ended up with an athlete or a doctor, that's why she kinda got into that field of work, unfortunately everyone was married and she wasn't trying to be no mistress, or a side anything. She was dating a hygienist but he got sued and lost everything including her. Jimmy just happened to be at the right place at the right time. She was just planning to date him until she scored a big fish but the heart is a tricky piece of work and Jimmy was a smooth talker with an anchor for a third leg. When he docks his boat he makes the bed rock. As she got older she started to realize that you're not going to get it all, so her best bet is to upgrade him and hold on tight.

She had to put her phone on silent because Crystal

was blowing her up. She definitely shouldn't have skipped work and gone with her to the Ramada. What Jimmy wont know wont hurt, right. She finished freshening up and walked out the bathroom into Jimmy's big arms. His cologne was even making her horny and he could read between the lines very well.

Took you long enough, it felt like forever. Let's go shower and change, everyone looks like they're going to the pool era. I hear music, I think it's a party. Jimmy started grinding his trunk on Debbies backside like he was making a baby throw her tights. As she was backing it up an older couple was looking at them like they needed to get a room. They danced to the elevators, got on and kissed all the way back to their room.

Jimmy looked off the Balcony as Debbie put on her bathing suit. Yeap party over here, look the whole resort is outside we probably the only 2 people in their room. He could hear the DJ cutting it up. He finally was going to get the opportunity to dance with his baby like he wanted to do at EVO. They hurried back downstairs with a complimentary bottle of 1800 from the bar in their suite. They got cranberry juice from a vending machine in the hallway, made an ice bag from the ice machine and it was on.

First friend they made was named Lucky. Lucky, the weed man, the tour guide, security for a nice tip he went and got food too. He was working the pool party and real recognize real so Jimmy gave him the street nod. Lucky knew what time it was and for the rest of the trip he was the guy. Lucky aint have no high grade but it didn't matter, so much liquor was flowing all Jimmy needed was a blunt to smoke to keep him in the zone.

The party was cracking, you had your bad girl crew from florida and your young thug click from New Orleans. Everyone else was couples, cougars and sugar daddies. The craziest mixed crowd Debbie has ever seen. She just kept laughing, Jimmy was blowing smoke in her face and lining up shots. Lucky even got lucky and got a little dance but Jimmy wasn't that drunk. He was watching them hands and palming her booty to let the fellas know she was about to be off the market permanently.

The night was so good they just woke up the next morning, Hang over wasn't even the word. Jimmy made coffee and ordered breakfast from room service. There was plenty to do but they had time. They kinda slept in the whole morning enjoying the room. Debbie wanted to have a nice dinner so she convinced him to get fly and pick the second restaurant and try their fine Mexican cuisine.

This time Jimmy just ordered a cheeseburger deluxe with bacon fried onions and Avocados. Debbie tried a soup and corn salad then she had a bean burrito that tasted like her mothers chilly and rice. She loved it but could only finish half. The rest she finished early in the morning when the munchies kicked in with Jimmy and that damn island weed.

They jet skied, rode horses, painted on the beach, went on a tour through ancient Mexican ruins that Lucky hooked them up with. Everything was going smooth the next 3 days until it wasn't.

They were in the room listening to Debbie's wireless

speaker. She jumped in the jacuzzi and didn't think twice of leaving her phone open playing on the bed next to her pillow. Jimmy didn't like that Beyonce Texas hold em song he wanted to listen to a mexican song Debbie downloaded the other day when they hit up the bar called El Jarabe Tapatio- The Mexican Hat Dance but it had a Hip-Hop street mix that was hot. They never locked their phones on one another so he could touch her shit, so he thought.

Jimmy grabbed the phone and proceeded to change the music, Crystal texted her some shit threw whats app that said, I can't wait to get you again, every time I think of you my body start throbbing, I miss you, text me back when you get a chance, I love you xoxo.

What the fuck shouted Jimmy at the top of his lungs. Debbie jumped out the water realizing her playlist stopped.

Too late, Jimmy was already looking at the naked pictures and reading the texts that go back like 2 weeks or more.

What the fuck is this Deb, come the fuck on, how long you 2 been messing around.

I can explain babe, give me my phone Debbie asked before Jimmy threw it into the Jacuzzi hot water.

She wouldn't stop, said Debbie, she rapped me at that party in the bathroom and I got her back.

Jimmy cut her off. He couldn't believe any of this. He wanted to beat Debbie's ass for lying all this time. He pulled the ring out from his hiding spot in his luggage, showed it to her and threw it off the balcony like Jake Cousins, Pitcher on the Yankees. He grabbed a bottle and walked out the room, leaving Debbie wet and Naked after diving for her phone.

Jimmy went down to the beach and hid, he didn't want no one to see him crying. He was so mad at all the sacrifices he made to please her. All the money he spent over the years, the losses he took. His cousin was still getting rich from the drug plug he set up. He did that bid, didn't take the money owed to him and walked away from that whole shit because he loved her so much. He started punching an old boat that was buried in the sand from years ago. He didn't know what else to do. He was sick and beside himself. All he could think about was Crystal all over his girl and she letting her like he was nothing. He couldn't understand, if she didn't love him she could have done it another way. He could have moved on, things were definitely about to change. This is so bad, he wanted to kill Debbie for hurting him like this. Tears then anger, tears then anger, he started seeing red taking a bottle of Jose Cuavo to the head wasn't helping the matter.

Finally he eased up a little when he saw some bad ass mommy's walk by. He went to talk with them and shared his bottle as he spilled his guts. They were team Jimmy all the way giving him encouragement and kisses on his cheek which gave him a little smile. Listen, life goes on, you are very handsome and I know your family loves you, just don't do anything stupid. It's still beautiful woman out there that treats men right, like us one of them said, rubbing him on his back. Here take my number, Jimmy stormed out the room and left his cellphone so she wrote it on his hand. My name is Isabella and I live in Cali if you're ever in my city. I just got divorced and I'm still looking for love. I didn't give up so you shouldn't either. Just go change your room, tell them the situation and get your bags out of her room and get some rest.

Great Idea, you know what would be even greater, if you girls keep me company. I need you, said Jimmy, holding on Isabella's arm.

Your lady aint going to find us and kill me, the ladies laughed.

Close one door then open the next, you got my number, use it. I'll answer.

You promise, I promise you I don't want you to harm yourself you got so much to live for, Isiablle took a good look at his package and sighed like she couldn't wait to get to know Jimmy better, and his friend. I love men, this my girl but we would never.

See you around we are leaving Friday, good luck!

They gave him one last kiss, Isabllea let him get a squeeze. It's real she said walking away swinging that cake making Jimmy feel like a man again. He went and did exactly what she said. He went to the front and the receptionist told him his wife was looking for him. He told her what happened and she changed his room with a promise that she wouldn't let Debbie know where they put him. She arranged to get his bags and transfer them to his new room when Debbie comes back to the lobby and they know she's not in the room.

Debbie was hysterical. She called and cursed Crystal the fuck out when she got her phone dry and operating again. She needed help finding Jimmy not knowing what he was capable of doing. She called Lucky and told him only what he needed to know. She couldn't find Jimmy and he's drunk out of his mind. Lucky went down one side of the beach and she went running down the other. They met back in the lobby about to alert the police. Debbie just was hoping Jimmy didn't wander off into the city; he may get robbed or worse. She was scared to death, all she wanted was to apologize and let Jimmy know how much she loved him and her and Crystal wasn't as serious as he's thinking.

The receptionist stopped her and told her she found Jimmy and he transferred rooms. They just went and got his bags. Unfortunately we can't tell you which room he told us about the situation and we can't allow fighting. The best we can do is give you the telephone number to his room but that is it. If you cause a commotion we may have to escort both you off the premises and you may have to pay for another Hotel until your flights back home are arranged.

Debbie was devastated. She didn't know what to do, if she leaves and goes home without Jimmy it's definitely over. If she stays and he tries to kill her, they may both go to jail in Mexico and don't nobody wants to go to jail in Mexico so she just went back to her room and sobbed until she got up the nerve to call him. He wasn't answering her calls because she found his phone charging in her bathroom. That was a good thing he may come and get it so she definitely will see him before they have to leave. She had all the flight info in her phone but Jimmy is unpredictable when he's mad, and she knew he was furious. Lucky escorted her back to her room and told her if he runs into him he would definitely call and let her know. She gave him a hefty tip for all his help then closed the door!

Debbie never felt so alone, she should've never let this happen. 5 years down the drain. Her whole family already thought they snuck off and got married. All she needed was a chance to make it up, she cried herself to sleep and prayed for a better day tomorrow. What a trip!

17

Jimmy woke up with a hangover, eyes bloodshot red from all the built up anger and frustration. He reached for his cellphone and remembered he didn't have it. Just when he was about to call the front desk the phone in his room rang.

Hello, Jim said thinking it was the receptionist from yesterday checking on him, nope it was Debbie.

Jimmy please don't hang up, you don't have to speak, just listen. I really have to apologize to you for everything and I'm asking you to please give me a second chance, I was so foolish and I will do anything to make this right. I don't want to lose 5 years like this, if you can please find it in your heart to forgive me. I will do anything baby please, she meant nothing to me, if you want me to transfer my job I will. I have your cell phone. I can bring it to you just tell me what to do.

Jimmy was silent then he thought about all they had been through and all she meant to him. So he told her to meet him in the back by the Gazebos. He wanted breakfast then they could talk there. He looked at his hand and wrote down Isabella's number, 2 can play this game he thought as he jumped in the shower for this confrontation.

Jimmy ate alone, then found Debbie standing with his cellphone and charger by the loveseats for couples only. She handed him his stuff then asked him to sit next to her. He stood as he looked in her eyes to see if another lie was going to spew out before he asked her his questions. So where does this leave us, and how the fuck can I trust you again. If i wouldn't have caught your slut phone on active this probably would have been going on for years as Crystal was about to be your best fucking friend right? You were about to get closer than close, then what? I totally trusted you and had my eyes closed. I was going to propose to you today and everything. Here's what's going to happen, this stupid clown vacation is done, when we get back home, i'm moving back to my moms house. I need some time, maybe then you and Crystal can work your thing out. Being that she loves you so much, lets not hurt her.

Debbie was trying to get some words in but Jimmy was heating up again. I don't want to hear shit. You and her owe me 10,000$ cash for my ring.

There is no me and her, only me and you, I will fix this. I swear to you I'm so, so sorry!

You're so, so sorry your conniving ass got caught. Lets book some flights outta here before i get locked up in Mexico and my parents have to come get me. Wait till I tell my moms this one. Debbie is the one Jim, you can't go wrong son, BULLSHIT!

Jimmy was ice cold all the way back home. He got separate seats on the plane and didn't dare to help Debbie with her thousand bags of luggage. He even hopped in a cab before her and left her at the airport looking stupid.

By the time Debbie got to the crib, Willow helped her upstairs as she came in crying.

Jimmy was already packing his things to leave again to his parents house. Debbie tried to talk to him but he bumped past Willow and skipped down the stairs to go to his new love, his Tahoe. Willow ran behind him!

Yo bro what's the deal, said Willow, grabbing Jimmy by his backpack.

No time right now lil bro, I'm done with her she is foul man.

Where are you going, y'all been together since I was yeah high. Gotta fix this, the cops were all over the ride but I saved you from getting tickets. When you come back you gotta take me for a spin around the block big homie.

Jimmy gave him a frustrated stair, I got you now move your scrawny ass out my way. I'll be at my moms House for a while. I'll text you the address, get you off this block. We can go to a game or something. Choose which one and call me.

Later, and you look out for her, she is still my wifey no matter how stupid she is, say less said Willow as Jimmy burned rubber while Debbie looked out the window depressed and confused on her next move, is she free or still in a relationship? She called her sister and began to unpack her and Jimmy's clothes. All his colognes, his wet gear she was remembering the few good days they had on the trip versus the bad ones. Her sister told her if it was meant to be it would work out and who the fuck is Crystal, she wanted to beat her ass she knew what she was doing getting in the middle of her sister life like that. She was more pissed at Debbie for letting it happen.

Look Sis you're more than welcome to come to my house and finish off your vacation. You know we love you down here anytime. She thanked her sister but another trip wasn't in her plans so she told her to give the kids her love and hang up.

Soon as she got up to go get a drink she felt a little bit of nausea coming on. She missed her period 2 weeks ago with so much going on she should have had it by now. She ran to the bathroom and threw up, grabbing her stomach. No it can't be, not right now Debbie screamed to herself as she looked for her pregnancy tester she brought a month ago. She was planning to ask Jimmy to go for it and see, maybe a baby would have been this new beginning she was really longing for. Jimmy not speaking to her, now how is this going to play out scratching her head in disbelief. Whatever happens she's keeping her baby but first this first. Time to piss on the stick and get these results.

Debbie finished unpacking and went to check the results. Pink, you pregnant Bi!%h now how the hell am I going to get Jimmy to believe this, he's going to think it's another man. Probably say it's Marvin's baby, me, him and Crystal got it on behind his back.

I totally fucked myself up with all this. She texted Jimmy please we have to talk but of course he did not respond so she called her cousin Adriona who lived in

Brooklyn to come over and help her sort this all out. Adriona and Debbie grew up together and called each other cousins from day one but they just lived on Morrison Avenue since 2. Jimmy hated Adriona because she kept trying to hook Debbie up with Ballers from her College that had their mommy and daddy money. Anyone that was going to inherit a fortune had their number in her purse trying to Get Debbie to help her double date. She only moved to Brooklyn chasing a Nets player who she married and divorced that same year when she realized he forced her to sign a prenup and not a Bently title when she was drunk after opening night and he scored 38 points against the Hawks.

Adriona came right away when she heard break up with Jimmy's broke ass. Tell me the good news,

I'm pregnant!

Awwww damn!

Not Jimmy's I hope, please tell me this about you cheating with a Doctor and Jimmy found out you got pregnant then he ran away back to his Mommy and Daddy.

Debbie sat her down and told her the whole ordeal. After she finished laughing from disbelief Adriona hugged her and told her whatever she needed she would provide and be there without hesitation like always, But Mr. Jimmy is going to want a DNA test asap before he goes for anything you tell him. You shore you just don't want to move in with me and start all over. I got a beautiful room for you and everything, you know I got you girl.

I'll keep that in mind but let's go get something to eat,

and you're coming with me to the hospital tomorrow so I can get a check up and more information for Jim.

You mean information to pin this baby on him so he could come home to your lying ass,

Awwww that's too cute, I guess I'm spending a night here, luckily I keep sleep over clothes in my trunk, you never know who man you gotta ride on a quick overnight.

And I'm the slut said Debbie, shaking her head and locking the door to the crib.

Jimmy went to his parents house across town in Throgs Neck where he grew up. She greeted him at the door with a big hug and made Jimmy drop his bags on the floor. Where's Mr Figueroa, your husband hiding? Down stairs in his man cave watching baseball as usual. Jimmy grabbed his stuff and went up to his room that was left spotless just the way he left it 6 years ago before he moved out. His weights, his twin size bed, his T.V and Stereo are all still operational. Mom still moped his floors every week like clock work. Home sweet home!

How long you staying said his mother reading something was seriously wrong with her baby.

I don't know mom, tell I know my next move I guess.

Dinner in 20 minutes, I made your favorite fried chicken, corn on the cob with white rice and cornbread.

Jimmy felt better already!

He unpacked his bags clearing out some of his drawers laughing at how skinny he was when he was younger. He didn't forget his money box, he wasn't leaving that for Debbie to find.

He put the money on the bed as his father walked in and closed the door behind him.

I knew you were in some shit, boy don't bring that drug money in my house, I done told you about this shit before, didn't I?

Hold on dad it's not at all what you are thinking, this aint drug money i promise you said Jimmy.

So why is it not in the bank where it belongs, that's where I got it from to be honest.

Jimmy sat his father down and explained everything up to this point of him being back home. His father was speechless and confused on how dumb his son could be.

You ain't get your brains from my side of the family. If you weren't my son I'd call the cops my goddamn self. Get your life together boy, put that money up before your mother sees it and I have to kick you outta here. How long are you staying? Doesn't matter you got 2 weeks to get this money out my house, you got any guns on you? NO! Any drugs up in here? NO!

Bet not, you ain't too old to see these hands you know I used to box, you remember, dont play with me, 2 weeks now fix it.

Jimmy pops turned, walked out and slammed the door leaving Jimmy in the room more stressed than ever. He checked his phone and Debbie was blowing him up. He keeped dubbing her, he didn't want to talk to her right now. His mother brought him his dinner and gave him a kiss goodnight like she always did before she went to bed. Talk to you tomorrow son, remember everyone makes mistakes and deserves a second chance. I took your father back when he was messing with your auntie, MOM I don't want to hear this right now. Jimmy interrupted her and started eating. We'll talk baby goodnight, I love you. I love you more my lady, sweet dreams Ma.

Debbie and Adriona were enjoying a seafood dinner at JP's in City Island. JP's crab legs and Jimbo Shrimp were hitting as the girls drank his signature drink called The Zombee they used to get twisted off of when they were younger. Debbie decided to get it in one last time knowing the Doctor was going to tell her to chill in the morning. No more drinks or hookah for nine months. Lord give me strength, she thought to herself. Adriona went to the bathroom as Debbie's phone was going off. It was Crystal texting and calling again, Debbie was buzzed and enjoying her time with her cousin so she blocked her.

The ladies paid the bill and were escorted out by JP himself. He remembered then and Debbie's Mom used to come through all the time.

By the time they arrived back at Debbie's crib to look for parking she saw Crystal double parked looking up at her front window playing Sexy Red blasting you my everything, leaning on her car hoping Debbie would come to her window since she blocked her calls.

Are you crazy, Debbie yelled as she got out of Adriona's vehicle going towards Crystal like she was about to knock her head off her shoulders. Crystal run around her car as Debbie yelled at her, it's over stay the fuck away from me you caused enough damage, I should have never let this go so far. Before Crystal could say I love you, she didn't see Adriona coming up behind her. You pregnant cuz I got this Bi!c#. Adriona grabbed her by her hair and proceeded to beat the brakes off Crystal's ass. Willow was loving every minute of it. He was recording until he heard the cops coming, then he broke it up and told Debbie to pull Adriona in the building, still kicking and swinging.

Crystal was dazed as they called the medics for her, she said she was okay as the cops asked Willow did he see who attacked her.

I just came outside, said Willow and she was like that on the floor. I don't know nothing officers, I live right here and I was going to the store for some juices for my mom and lil bro.

Crystal gathered herself and said she was alright, the ambulance came and took her in for further evaluation as the cops told her they had to tow her vehicle and she could pick it up when she was capable at the pound.

18

Debbie and Adriona came back out when they left and Debbie gave Willow a big hug for looking out. Adriona had a few cuts from her rings so they went upstairs to get her cleaned and bandaged up. I told her this was going to end badly for her. If she talks then imma talk and we both gonna go to jail. The girls went back down to the store to get some beers and chilled outside with Willow in the front of the building drinking and laughing. They even took him to go get something to eat. He played them all his tracks and the night ended like a normal summer night outside in front of the building like the old days. Music, conversation, and drinks!

Jimmy called his job and told them he was coming in today. He couldn't just stay hiding in his parents house, he just kept thinking about how Debbie played him. He had mixed feelings, it's not like it was a dude but still she gave herself to someone else. For some reason men can't sit and soak in their own misery. They have to stay productive so at this point Jimmy was ready to face whatever was coming his way, I mean what else can possibly make his life any worse at this point.

Jimmy got dressed in his clean and pressed uniform. Eric was happy to see him because it was a lot going down. Miss Helen wanted to see him right away to tell him the good news. Good news Jimmy thought to himself as he walked to the back to Miss Helen's corner little hut of an office.

Jimmy you came back so early from Mexico, how was it? She asked, not really caring. Guess what, the system is back as you know and we caught them. T and T Tanisha and Thomas were cashing blank checks from one of our prestigious customers' accounts. They took a little over 200 thousand dollars. We ain't proven it yet .but they are both under full investigation and will be charged by the Feds for there crimes. This is Mr. Hindenburg, who looked and gave a fake nod not trusting no one at this point. And we are in the process of reimbursing his money because it was fully secured and ensured, Helen continued. She pulled Jimmy to the side and whispered, Eric and I just calmed him down. Just stand outside and post up just in case I need you, OK DEAR that will be all, I'll talk to you in a minute let me finish up with Mr Hindenburg. It's good to see you, same to you said Jimmy as he left to post up outside her office just in case shit got crazy.

When the client left Miss Helen let Eric go home and Jimmy went to clean out the restroom to start his shift. He dropped to his knees and thanked God he didn't get in trouble he was off the hook so he thought.

A customer came in and helped him off the floor. I had to clean up some mess down there. Then he slid out the door to organize the crowd and get accustomed back to his regular routine. The smile on his face for the rest of the day was priceless. He was going to do a lot with that money to change his life. Real-estate here i come!

When Jimmy got home to his old room. He was tired as hell and just wanted to sleep but he couldn't. He put his headphones on and proceeded to listen to his playlist on his phone. A call came through from a number he didn't recognize. He thought it was Debbie playing more games so he didn't answer. He listened to the whole Pop Smoke album before he finally went to sleep.

Early morning piss hit him like a racehorse in the Kentucky Derby. He sat back on the bed and the number rang up again.

Look Debbie I know this is you, call Crystal what the fuck you calling me for.

The voice on the other line said, I'm not your Bi!c# money.

Jimmy was taken back as cool as he was today. Somebody must be crazy to talk to him like that.

Who the fuck is this? And why are you calling me at 3 in the morning when I don't know you.

The voice replayed, you can call me Dodge and you have to get to know me quickly because I need my money asap.

What money? Jimmy said, confused who knows about his stash.

Dodge broke down all the figures to every amount the

ATM machines spit out since day one. He knew the time and the number on the machines that malfunctioned.

Jimmy was scratching his head, I don't know what you're talking about and how you got my number but I ain't got time for this right now. Before Jimmy could bang the line, Dodge shouted out, well I hope you're ready for jail because I got you on video scooping the money up and taking it home. 555 East Tremont Ave apartment 4B, Jimmy Figueroa, wifey Debbie Washington, Right?

Jimmy almost dropped his phone, who the fuck is this man with all his information, he got everything but his social he thought getting annoyed of the BS that been happening to him all week.

Ight, said Jimmy you got my attention.

Met me tomorrow at Popeyes on 400 East Tremont. Let's have lunch not far from you so don't be late 2 o'clock sharp.

I know it, said Jimmy getting heated up about all the events happening to him so fast in the last 3 days.

If you don't show, you better move because your girl looks mighty fine and I love me a Fat ass, after I take care of her these videos will be dropped off at the Precinct.

How will I recognize you? said Jimmy.

I'll be wearing a Yankee cap and a gray hoodie. You won't miss me, it's popeyes and I don't look like a Bass Head. Dodge banged the phone.

Debbie woke up and made Adriona breakfast for fighting for her last night. They didn't get into anything like that in years. Brought back a lot of childhood memories all they were missing was her sister who she couldn't wait to tell she was pregnant after this Doctor's visit today.

Debbie Knew all the Doctors in the whole facility. She liked Doctor Ciara the most, Adriona waited outside until she saw a Doctor of her own to check out her Uterus. She stuck her head in the room and told Debbie she'd be right back, going to get lunch in the cafeteria with Dr Shear M.D. Debbie just shook her head as she continued to get her blood work and urine sample. Dr Ciara gave her the whole run down all the nooks and crannies she needed to know to start her pregnancy journey. 6 to 8 days come in or call me for the results of the blood work. If you feel anything uncomfortable come in right away to see me, otherwise you're fine and congratulations, said Dr Ciara who had a dozen patients waiting for her in the waiting room so she had to go.

Adriona was supposed to be there for support but she really wished Jimmy was there because he was the father. She was just giving him time to cool off. Once she tells him she is pregnant she feels he's going to forgive but never forget Jimmy never forgets anything. One time she got this guy's number just so he could stop flirting with her. She never was going to call him but Jimmy found the number doing laundry and he never lets her forget about that and that was 4 years ago.

After the appointment Debbie had to find Adriona. She called her over the loudspeaker, Paging Dr Adriona. You are wanted in the parking lot. It's time to go your cousin is tired and pregnant, bring your butt back to the waiting area.

Adriona came running, laughing her head off and congratulating Debbie because they are both about to have a new baby. What's the Gender you can't see that yet, but I feel like it's going to be a boy. Jimmy always wanted a son, said Debbie worried about how she's going to break him the news. How I'm I going to get this man back?

First off you gotta try to keep your legs closed and your tongue in your mouth, said Adriona giggling frantically.

Debbie made such a sharp stair, she could've cut her head off. He blocked my ass. I called him so much yesterday.

Call his mother and tell her. No, he probably told them everything and they hate me by now. Write him a letter and mail it, what if he doesn't open it he knows my hand writing. Go over there and bang on the door, I'll take you. You just want to see me get slapped. I wish they would, said Adriona, cracking her knuckles. I'll beat Mrs Figueroa old ass up. Get a baby on board shirt, go to his job and take him some lunch rubbing your belly. That's actually not a bad idea. I'm going to give him a little more time then I'm going to do that. He's not going to kill me at his job I hope.

Dodge was waiting for Jimmy who was like 10 minutes late. He had to have a middle man because he was about to make a phone call. Jimmy was watching him through the window to make sure he was alone. Jimmy walked in and Dodge ordered him to buy a six piece special they could share. Dodge looked like he did some time but he also looked like he had an education. 2 ice teas too, it's hot today. Jimmy did as he was told not knowing what to expect so the first thing he did was drink down his beverage because he was starting to sweat a little bit.

Sup, said Jimmy trying to keep his composure because he's a fighter but he can tell Dodge had a hammer in his sweater pointed at Jimmy under the table. He grabbed everything with his left hand and didn't lift up his right the whole time. Sit down, take a look at the phone and press play. Jimmy saw like 4 videos of him taking the cash off the ground from the machines and stuffing them in his work bag. The video was thrown through the window of the bank so Dodge or someone was watching him from the outside.

I don't want to put you in jail or harm any of your loved ones. I used to work for a technical system programming company that wired cameras in all the banks downtown. I'm also a hacker and I hacked into the ATM machines by shooting a virus into the system. Basically I gave the ATM devices a flu and made it cough up the cash. I needed someone in the Bank that works nights because it's less people and your site was perfect because my informant let me know that you shut down and lock up the Bank at 12. My company got sued because a lot of us were hitting Banks and we slipped up and one of my partners got caught and snitched. That's why all the Banks shut our systems down and hired a new company. Thank God I managed to put this plan into play before they got a new on guard system put in to catch hackers. I believe you still have my cash, I just want my 200 thousand and you can have the rest. Please don't tell me you spent it, I don't have a problem popping you right here, right now.

Dodge put the gun on Jimmy's knee to let him know it's not a game. Slide me the phone back, go get my money and I'll meet you by your crib tonight at 10 o'clock. No cash and trust me you won't see it coming. Debbie will meet you in the afterlife so you won't be alone, don't play with me fam 10 o'clock, bring me my bag and you can go on with your life. Now get up and ask them to open the bathroom, go in, close the door, turn off the light then count to twenty. When I see the light go out, I'll leave, you turn that knob and I'm shooting through that door. He banged the nozzle on Jimmy's knee to make him move and listen.

Jimmy did as he was told as he came out he ran outside to see if he saw a car pull off or Dodge walking with someone he knew. An informant, he would bet his money on Eric. He is the only one that knows everything about him. They worked together for years and even hung out together. Debbie knows his wife and kids but why, we argue but get me killed when this is done imma kill Eric ass I swear to God. He better not have anything to do with this.

Jimmy called Eric 4 times and he didn't answer, He texted him. Do you know anybody named Dodge? Hit me back asap I dont give a fuck what your doing hit me NOW!

Jimmy drove to his block to see if Debbie was alright. He went upstairs to see if she was home. She wasn't so he unblocked her but didn't want to bother her with this situation unless he had to. He went downstairs to look for

Willow. He was about to go gather up the cash but he had to see Willow so he called him.

Where are you at?

With my brother at his basketball game, Willow said. Why, what's up?

I'm in some shit and I need you to be around at about 9 o'clock, talk to you then. If you see Debbie tell her I came by and then tell her I said go to her mothers house until I call her. Tell her I forgive her but leave, no games life or death. Make sure you tell her it's not a game. LEAVE!

Jimmy went to his moms house in a mad panic. His mother went to church and his father was with his drinking buddy that lived next door. He knew because he smelled Champagne cologne the only one Mr Frank wears and he definitely came over to get pops to go drink and talk sports. They have been doing that for more than twenty years. Moms won't be home until 6 so he had time to count that money up and hit the road.

Jimmy was mad he had to give up this money all he went through but he also knew it was burning his soul to have it. He didn't want to play with Dodge and his life so he decided to fight fire with fire. He went to his pops stash and got old Betty his pops 38 revolver he uses to protect his house. Pops kicked his cousin out with her one time when he was running from the law and he tried to spend a night but his sister already called and told him Chris was on the run. Pops grabbed that 38 and escorted his ass off his promises like he was a stranger

Jimmy loaded it up and put it in his glove compartment

so he wouldn't leave without it. Threw the 200 in the back seat then called Willow.

Did you see Debbie, yeah she was with Adriona mad cool chick I told her what you said and she went upstairs then left with her for her mothers house. She told me to tell you sorry, she kept saying that then she said for you to call her when you get to the crib so she could come home and see you.

What the fuck is going on big bro you got me like worried. Is it cops, is it beef, you want me to call my Goonies? We got your back, ain't nothing I'm bout that life said Willow super serious.

I'm on my way now. As soon as I get there imma tell you what to do.

Debbie called him but he just wanted to stay focused because shit was about to go down. He is gonna give Dodge the money but he needs to get them videos in that cell phone erased or he can keep black mailing him for the rest of his life. He definitely wanted to keep some of the money so he could move. He left a couple of thousand at his moms house but his plan is to ask Dodge for at least another 20,000$ because he made some plans and he knows what he looks like too so we all can go to jail, fuck it. He ain't doing all this for nothing, a truck and a downpayment on a house was a good deal for all his stress, pain and suffering.

Jimmy parked his truck on the corner of his block, called Willow again and told him to get in so they could talk.

Jimmy gave Willow a quick run down, you about this

like I need you to help me get this gun off this dude named
Dodge coming to get 200 thousand from me at 10 o'clock.

The plan is imma give you my gun right, you listening?
I need you to be on point. Have you ever shot a gun before?
Yeah, I got you, said Willow. You may not need to but if I
give you a head nod pop that mother fucker, I'll take the
charge but I dont think its going to go that far. All I need is
time. You go up behind him and surprise him because he
thinks I'm going to be alone. Imma tell him what I need to
tell him, give him the bag, take his gun from him and

his cell phone, I gotta get that, then we gonna kick him
the fuck off our block.

Jimmy repeated it to Willow 3 times, then he called
Debbie just to hear her voice.

Debbie answered on the first ring,

Jimmy I was so terrified you said no games. That
means this is serious, you can't go back to jail because
you're pregnant, I mean I'm pregnant you're going to be a
father.

Yeah mother fucker, its yours too so dont talk no shit,
said Adriona in the background.

Turn your dog off Debbie, and stop playing with me
you don't have to lie to get me back, ain't no time for the
games right now.

She walked away from Adriona, I'm having your baby
Jim. You're going to be a father, my baby daddy.

I'll call you back!

Jimmy got out of the truck and walked back and forth
as he told Willow the good news. Now he needs more than

20$. He's going to have a kid, he has to ask for 50$, but first he has to get that cellphone and destroy it.

It's 9 o'clock, you stay in the truck and duck down. Imma wait for him in front of the building when he comes for the money imma make him turn his back your way. Just creep up and stick it in his back and I'll do the rest, but you gotta make sure he feels the pistol.

GOT IT!

Jimmy was nervous as hell, now he has something to live for so at the end of the day he's going to give Dodge the cash without a doubt. If he dont want to let nothing extra go, fuck it but he needs that cellphone in his hand before he leaves.

It was people outside so was Dodge gonna go crazy and pop off likely not.

10 o'clock came and Dodge came down the block walking with a Boo Shiesty on covering his face to let Jimmy know he's with the smoke. He walked straight up to Jimmy as Jimmy met him and turned him in the right direction so his back was to the corner where his truck was parked.

Dodge broke the ice, is the money all there?

Jimmy kindly asked him, do you have the cellphone and can you show me if it's the same one from earlier?

You think this is a game, he went to reach for the gun from behind his back but Willow stuck him with the revolver and said put you hands the fuck up. Caught Dodge way off guard he thought he scared Jimmy enough to come alone with all the cash.

Jimmy yelled change of plans, he took the gun from Dodge back and told him to give him the cellphone. Willow dug his pockets and found the cell phone as he went to pass it to Jimmy, Dodge tested their gangster and turned around and knocked Willow out as the gun went off, Willow shot Dodge in his back and hit the ground out cold. Dodge still managed to knock the gun out of Jimmy's hand as he took off with the cellphone and the money he turned straight into the arms of another man with a face mask on in front of the laundromat.

Pow the man shot Jimmy in the stomach and took the bag of money out his hand. Jimmy managed to pull his mask off as he fell to the ground.

ARTY you mother fucker!

Pow, Pow he shot Jimmy 2 more times at close range, ran to help Dodge to his feet and kicked Willow in his head who was already knocked out on the ground then fled to a car they had already parked around the corner for the getaway.

Mr Jeff, Jr and everyone in the Laundromat came out to their aid. Jr called an Ambulance and the cops while Mr. Jeff was trying to stop Jimmy's bleeding with towels and sheets from his dry cleaning bag. Jimmy pulled out his truck keys and said Debbie and the baby. Then dropped in Mr. Jeff's arms. There was blood everywhere the Ambulance came pretty quickly but to no avail Jimmy bleed out on his own block. In front of all his neighbors and friends in a pool of his own blood.

The cops took his cell phone for evidence, Debbie was calling and texting all night. The police answered and told her the bad, heartbreaking news. She fell to the ground and Adriona took the phone and got the rest of the information. She told the family before the cops did as they all met up to view the body. His parents found out they lost a kid and got one on the same day.

THE FUTURE

Jimmy Figuroea Jr was born 7 pounds 11 ounces, and looked like all his fathers baby pictures.

Debbie and Mrs Gwen spoiled that baby so bad he had 200 thousand in the bank by the time he was 10. Debbie is leading by example and teaching him how to make great choices in his life, work hard and don't ever take anything you didnt work hard for, always tell the truth and don't keep no secrets from your family. If you are going through anything we work it out together as a family. 10 heads are better than one.

Jimmy died for nothing, resting in his grave. Never got a chance to get married, meet his kid, start a business or write a WILL to secure his family's future. You think when he woke up that morning he knew he was going to die that night, Life is too unpredictable. If you put yourself in positions where things can go wrong, they will, We gotta stop taking chances and make guarantees. Stop living on doubt and praying on hope. You can't dream big with your hand out. I know a lot of Jimmys, NO DIDDY BOP! With one life to live, don't waste your time, you'll never get it back and your past doesn't necessarily have to dictate your future. Learn all those lessons and create a brighter you, then have a kid for a greater you.

FACTS

Black on black crime these days is the leading cause of death among young black men, and contributes significantly to the shortened life-span of the Black male. In about 80-90% of these cases, the Black victim was killed by another Black, and about 52% of murder victims are psychologically impaired, we must acknowledge that a murder is similarly impaired and Blacks for both environmental and political reasons are likely to reflect emotional predispositions that allow them to more readily become a homicide statistic. Projected self-hatred facilitates blind rage and gives the perpetrator of the violence attack a sense of legitimacy and justification. In addition, Blacks have been indoctrinated by a criminal justice system which places higher value on a White life than on a Black life.

THE TRUTH

I wrote this story to show the reader that people that grow up in a poverty type environment tend to not only be poor but also make poor life choices. Instead of doing the right thing they will risk it all and make choices that in the long run will cost them their lives or put them in jail. Why does it take so long for a black man to accumulate wealth? You have to check your history. What are we missing? I say it's inheritance from our broken parents and inheritance from theirs. We never ever get a break because a lot of us are born already in the mud. I don't think people should have children if they don't have the resources to take care of them, but we do, and they suffer just like we did when we were young and our parents did when they were young. It's a cycle that has to be broken by knowledge and under-standing.

Something as simple as a Will could change this minority game of life. The white man makes a Will that orchestrates instructions to his family to keep the wealth in the family for generations and generations to come. That's why they have all the land, all the gold, all the resources to stay on top. We make businesses that the government allows us to open with a large quantity of rules that if broken we lose it all just as fast if not faster then we got it. Is that fair? If Jimmy's father would have accumulated wealth from his father or land from his fathers father you think Jimmy would have worked at a bank and taken money or would he have had the opportunity to own one?

EVOLUTION

What if? Is the biggest question in the world. What if we were not taken from our land and brought here as slaves. What if our ancestors were rich and they created Wills for use to keep our wealth. We would never know because our legacies were stolen and our histories were rewritten and now we live in the land of the lost where we're controlled like puppets on a string. What can we do to change our dynamics? We must join forces to get our wealth back and create Wills to keep control of it for our future generations' security. How many people you know that wrote a Will, don't worry ill wait. Tupac said it best. We gotta change the way we eat, we gotta change the way we live, and we gotta change the way we treat each other to survive and look at what happened to him. I wonder if he got a chance to write a Will, I doubt it.

I just wrote this to bring light to the game that we sleep on. Our DNA from past to present will never be strong as silk. A lot of people died for us to be here and how we pay them back by not having respect for that and allowing the white man ancestors to laugh at us because they are still winning. Every time we take a life we're doing their job for them now sit back and smoke on the if you Will.

ACKNOWLEDGMENTS

Peace and Love!

I would like to take this time out to thank all my readers without you guys none of this would be possible for me. I hope my words greet you in the best of health and the story I told doesn't offend anyone. This story is fictional I freestyled it off the top of my dome piece, I used to be a rapper but I always been a writer my brian is kinda eclectic like that. I channel on all the gifts God gave me for the win and I thank you for helping me achieve one of my dreams. I aim to please with much more to come God willing!

Endless LOVE,

BOO,

That's my name, NO DIDDY BOPPIN!

CHURCH!

.

www.ingramcontent.com/pod-product-compliance
Lightning Source LLC
Chambersburg PA
CBHW071338150726
47997CB00002B/778